Cam

8 Simple Rules for Dating My Teenage Daughter

And other tips from a
beleaguered father
(not that any of them work)

By W. Bruce Cameron

WORKMAN PUBLISHING • NEW YORK

*To my wife, Mary Ellen,
without whom I would not be
the father of teenage daughters.*

Copyright © 2001 by W. Bruce Cameron

Library of Congress Cataloging-in-Publication Data

Cameron, W. Bruce.
  8 simple rules for dating my teenage daughter : and other tips from a beleaguered
  father, not than any of them work / by W. Bruce Cameron
     p. cm.
  ISBN 0-7611-2314-8
   1. Adolescence—Humor. 2. Parenting—Humor. 3. Dating (Social customs)—
  Humor. I. Title: Eight simple rules for dating my teenage daughter. II. Title.

  PN6231.A26 C36 2001
  814'.6—dc21   2001017692

Cover photograph by Tony Loew
Cover design by Paul Gamarello
Book design by Lisa Hollander

Workman Publishing Company, Inc.
708 Broadway
New York, NY 10003-9555
www.workman.com

Printed in the United States of America

First printing March 2001
10 9 8 7 6 5 4 3 2 1

CONTENTS

A Stiff
Dose
of Reality

By the Time You Realize You're Living with a Teenage Daughter, It's Too Late

Not that it makes a whole lot of difference now, but I never intended to be the father of two teenage daughters. I suppose if I had been asked, I might have chosen to go with something cheaper, like a stable of race-horses, or something easier to raise, like wolverines. But the question my wife put to me was couched in such innocent language, I simply didn't consider the ramifications. Plus, she had surprised me by preparing a candlelight dinner, pouring me wine, and wearing something rather distracting—to this day, I don't remember what we ate. (Wives probably go to a special school to learn tactics like this.) I *do* remember what she said, which was, "Don't you think it's time we thought about starting a family?"

"Sure!" I recall answering with an enthusiasm appropriate to both the situation and the manner in which she was attired. I could see no harm in *thinking* about starting anything. I thought about starting stuff all the time. I was even encouraged in this pursuit by my wife, who handed me lists of projects to think about starting every weekend.

(This endearing little game—her giving me a list, and my falling asleep on the couch—is one of the things she still enjoys most about our relationship.)

Thus we began the period in our marriage I've come to remember rather fondly as the "breeding frenzy."

"Do you think you could put off cutting the lawn this morning? I may be ovulating," my wife would say.

"All right, just this once," I would sigh.

Of course, once the novelty wore off, I felt that I had become a dehumanized sex unit whose primary function was impregnation. I was at the absolute beck and call of my spouse, who demanded my complete surrender to her singular desire to become with child and who had no compunction whatsoever about interrupting whatever I was doing to summon me to bed for another try.

I've never been happier in my life.

When I look back on it, I suppose I should have thought about the possibility that what we were doing could, eventually, produce a teenage daughter. But in my defense, men who are in the middle of a breeding frenzy don't have a lot of extra brain cells to spare for pondering stuff like that. Besides, my wife, who used to *be* a teenage daughter and should have known better and I will always blame her for this, never once introduced the notion into our conversations. When she mentioned anything at all, it was about this *family* we were thinking about starting. She never even used the word "baby" in my presence.

During the breeding frenzy, my wife and I purchased caseloads of home pregnancy tests (HPTs). These cute little devices replace the old method of making an appointment with the doctor, having a blood test, and then waiting to find out if, for reasons never fully explained, one of the doctor's pet rabbits died. An HPT can cut short the breeding frenzy by more than two weeks, which leads me to conclude that they were *not* invented by men.

When our HPT finally turned out positive, I did my best to look pleased that we could stop breeding. (My argument that the activities should continue for a while longer "to assure total victory" was completely ignored by my wife, proving that women just don't understand sports analogies.)

"It's a Girl!"

I was thrilled the day we brought our little infant home from the hospital and put her in the crib I had spent eight hours assembling. It was a unique and complicated piece of furniture, with sides that fell off at the pull of a spring-loaded latch. (Later my father-in-law came over and jury-rigged the sides so that they remained attached and slid up and down on rails. For the sake of peace in the family, I didn't point out how boring this was.)

Soon after daughter number one, we had number two, and a few years later, a boy. What in God's name were we thinking? Perhaps we simply couldn't conceive of any process powerful enough to turn our adorable little babies into teenagers. But despite our best efforts, it happened.

My older daughter apparently feels that because she was born first, she needs to do everything she can to maintain her lead, even though neither of my other two children is aware there's even a contest. The word "competitive" (awarded her by a kindergarten teacher who was dismayed when my daughter took down everyone else's artwork from the class bulletin board) seems somehow inadequate to describe her—probably "take no prisoners" comes closer. Her schedule is full of athletic and social events for which the entire family is expected to make room. In her view, I am at my best when I am lugging her volleyball gear to the car or giving her money to attend a pep club dinner.

She believes that her driver's license is her own personal Emancipation Proclamation, freeing her from all familial duties. Her room looks like a documentary about the effects of wind shear on the teenage bedroom. Her friends' fathers are all much more successful than I at extracting material gain from the free enterprise system, but she doesn't want anyone to know this, so she disguises my modest means behind a cleverly constructed campaign of capricious expenditure.

Yet despite her lifelong rebellion against my reasonable rules, she will spontaneously hug me when I least expect it, a simple gesture that sometimes leaves me speechless.

My middle child came into the world, took a look at my older daughter, and decided that no matter what, she would Not Be Like Her. She's much more moody, always seeking to locate that dark cloud hovering over the silver lining. She does well in school and also plays volleyball—but she doesn't want to talk about it. Given the chance, she would take her meals through a slit in her door and interact with her parents only on Christmas.

She's informed me she is saving for a Harley-Davidson motorcycle and a boa constrictor. She doesn't even blink when I refer to her unwashed friends collectively as "the Manson family." In fact, she rarely registers that I am even talking to her.

Yet she is also the daughter who ends her notes to me with, "I love you, Dad." As in, "Dear Dad, I took the car, I hope you weren't planning to do anything with it today. I'll call in six hours to see if you need it back. I love you, Dad. Bye."

Cynics might suspect that my girls' inconsistent behavior is merely part of a devious campaign to keep me off balance and vulnerable, but I don't think so. As much as I am struggling with them, I think my teenagers are struggling with themselves, trying to figure out who they are going to be when they grow up. Which is silly—why don't they just ask me?

My youngest is a completely disinterested boy who hasn't yet shown any signs of preteen syndrome. He regards his sisters as some sort of science experiment gone awry, and sees no practical purpose in them whatsoever. His relationship isn't so much hostile as apathetic because, well, they're girls.

My wife and I often talk about how wonderful it was when our children were babies, though she usually frowns at me when I demand to know what we did wrong that they grew up. Things were going so well for a while there! (I manfully assume a lot of the blame myself, pointing out that I am not perfect and thus married a woman who makes mistakes. She takes little comfort in my magnanimous concessions, only asking if I remember when our children "were such cute little babies.")

Yes, I remember, but I don't see the relevance. Babies are to teenagers what a puppy is to a werewolf. Babies love you and cling to you and want to be with you. Teenagers want you to drop them at the movies with your face averted or maybe in a paper bag, so their friends will think they were beamed down by the starship *Enterprise* and are not in any way the product of parental activity. Babies are characterized by what they can't do: can't walk, can't talk, can't leave the room when you start to explain why life was so much harder when *you* were growing up. For teenagers, it's what they *won't* do: won't clean their rooms, won't get off the phone, won't listen when you start to explain why life was so much harder when *you* were growing up.

"How do you survive with two teenage daughters?" I was once asked.

"I'm surviving?" I responded, amazed.

A Father's Guide to the Impossible

Studies show that the world population of teenagers is on the rise, and I'm convinced that every single one of them comes over to my house after school to eat my food. (My wife ignores my instructions and actually spends money trying to satisfy these adolescent appetites, which is a bit like trying to warm a winter day by turning up the heat and opening your windows.)

Anyway, the world is positively teeming with teenagers, and as long as people continue to "think" about starting a family, the trend is likely to continue. This is not my fault. I am willing to accept the blame only for the ones that my wife caused. But if I am, indeed, surviving the experience, perhaps I can share with you some of the knowledge I have so painfully gained over what has been more than half a decade of tears, hormones, and stress fractures. If you've had a baby or are engaged in breeding, I will tell you what you have to look forward to. If it's been about a dozen birthdays since you brought home that darling little bundle of girl baby, I am willing to explain the skills and tactics you will need to make it through the next eight years with a minimum of trauma.

Having a child mutate into a teenager is a bit like being an airline passenger who must suddenly take over for a stricken pilot and land the plane. And in this case, the passengers are all yelling, "I hate you! I hate you!" and slamming the door to the cockpit.

With a book like this—an "owner's manual," if you will—you may learn enough to make it to the airport safely. Otherwise, you might as well go back and finish watching the movie with everybody else.

The Gathering Storm

First things first. Let's diagnose the situation. Just because your blood pressure is so high you swear other people can *hear* it doesn't mean you're suffering from teenager—your daughter might be a preteen, which is sort of like having a tornado before a hurricane hits. Here's a checklist that you can use to confirm your worst fears.

Warning Signs That You May Be Living with a Teenage Daughter

- Your phone is always busy, so you put in a second line, and it's always busy.
- Your gas tank is always empty and your laundry basket is always full.
- While you've generally been in favor of them up until now, suddenly Miracle Bras seem like a really bad idea.
- You realize it's been more than a year since you haven't had to pay a late fee when you rent a video.
- Your car insurance suddenly costs more than your car.

If you are experiencing some of the above warning signs, *do not panic*. Follow the advice contained in this book and remain focused on your goal, which is to get the teenagers moved out of the house before *they* breed and the whole cycle begins again. (Some sociologists decry the loss of the "generational home," where grandparents, parents, and children all live under the same roof. I've never heard such nonsense in my life.)

Remember, *you can get through this*. Your parents did, which is why they always start laughing when you call to explain to them how impossible it is to live with teenage daughters. (If, as they are choking through their hilarity at your expense, they claim that your child's behavior sounds "just like *you* at that age," hang up immediately. Not only is this completely ridiculous, but if you allow your parents to express this thesis, they will become obsessed with the idea, and that's all you'll hear for the next decade.)

I Need You, Leave Me Alone

When children are young, dads regard themselves as giant shock absorbers, there to protect the family from the ruts and bumps on the road of life. But gradually, the role of the father evolves. You begin to see yourself as more like a coach, running your children through practice drills so they'll be better prepared when they have to go out and play the real game. Life's a contact sport, dads will argue, so a few nonfatal bruises along the way merely toughen the body and steel the soul. If a daughter fails to save enough money to purchase a homecoming dress, why then, she doesn't get a homecoming dress! (Naturally, no one else in the family agrees with this.)

There are a few exceptions to this now-is-the-time-to-experience-some-of-life's-pitfalls philosophy: some calamities, such as teenage boys, are viewed as still too dangerous for your daughters in all but the most controlled situations. And these are the very experiences your daughters will most crave, thrusting the father-daughter relationship into a series of battles that can be summed up as the father saying, *"I can't help you out of every unfortunate situation you get yourself into. You need to do things on your own now, except for when I don't want you to."*

On the other side of the battle zone, your daughter is saying, *"I don't need your advice. I don't want your rules. I am an adult. I am completely independent. I need money for lunch."*

Now What?

Having a teenage daughter puts you in what is commonly referred to as a "punting situation." However, there is no receiving team on the field, so you're going to have to carry the ball yourself. It's not going to be easy—in fact, I'm pretty sure it's impossible. But no one else is going to do it: you've got to, you're the father.

The Gulf of Communications

A Guide for Conversing with Teenage Daughters for Those Times When It Is Simply Unavoidable

When nations go to war with one another, they are courteous enough to serve unambiguous notice. After Pearl Harbor, as an example, I don't imagine that the president and his advisers sat around saying, "What the heck do you suppose they meant by *that*?" But when a daughter decides to become a teenager, she does so in secret conspiracy, deliberately choosing not to advise you she has decided it's time to take over the family and run it her way.

The first signs of adolescence are not physical, they're mental: *you* begin to go crazy. Your daughter doesn't appear one morning wearing a button that says, NOW BEHAVING IRRATIONALLY, HAVE A NICE DAY.

Instead, she comes down to breakfast and says, "Do you have any *idea* how sickening it is to come downstairs and see you sitting there eating eggs every single morning?"

Fathers are to be forgiven if they try to figure out what this means. Is it the act of coming downstairs that causes this acute bout of sickness? Is it the mere fact that it is you who are sitting there? Is it the eating, or maybe the eating of eggs? Or is it just that this occurs every morning?

"Forget it," your daughter will non-answer, by which she means yes, yes, yes, and yes. You've been given notice, subtle as a subpoena: she's becoming a teenager.

During her teenage years, a daughter's brain undergoes changes that are, for the most part, completely unacceptable to a father. Apparently there is some sort of gland that begins dumping hormonal pollution into a daughter's bloodstream at age twelve or so, though why medical science has been unable to locate and eliminate this gland, I will never understand. Thus stimulated by these hormones or germs or whatever they are, the female teenage brain calls a team meeting of the senses to hand out new operating instructions.

> **Female Teenage Brain:** Okay, Senses, settle down and listen up. I want to effect some drastic changes in the way we've been doing things around here. Sight?
> **Sight:** Yes ma'am?
> **Female Teenage Brain:** I want you to concentrate on two things: your immediate peer group and Brad Pitt. You know that guy who used to lean into our crib and make those nauseating kissing noises at us when we were too little to tell him to go away?

Sight: Father?

Female Teenage Brain: That's the one. Do your best not to look him directly in the eye anymore. And let us know when you spot him coming because . . . Hearing, you listening?

Hearing: What else would I be doing?

Female Teenage Brain: I like that snotty attitude, Hearing. You're going to go far in this organization!

Hearing: Thank you, ma'am.

Female Teenage Brain: When Sight has this father character in our scopes, I want you to shut down completely.

Hearing: But he has such wise things to say!

Female Teenage Brain: That's what we used to think, but not anymore. Speech, these changes will really affect you, are you ready?

Speech: Yes ma'am!

Female Teenage Brain: That's the spirit. I need a ten-fold increase in word production out of you, effective immediately.

Speech: But . . . but what will I say?

Female Teenage Brain: It doesn't matter, just keep the words coming. We recently got in a few million copies of the word "like," plus a whole shipment of "ohmygod." If you can't think of anything else, use them.

Speech: Like, ohmygod, you mean, like, I should be, like . . . like this?

Female Teenage Brain: Perfect.

Most of the verbal output from a teenager is discharged into the telephone system, though computer companies have recently put "chat" technology into American homes to help handle some of the load. This makes telephone companies happy because it means we now must all pay for two lines going into our houses, so that our daughters can chat on the PC while they simultaneously output into the phone.

"Ohmygod, Amanda, what you just wrote is, like, so hilarious," my older daughter will gush into the phone as she types, *AMANDA, THIS IS HILARIOUS.* I peer over her shoulder at the monitor. *LOL. ROFL. ROFLMA*, she types, which is code for "Let's drive my father crazy with chat technology."

"I need to use the phone," I tell her.

"But Dad, I am working on my *homework*," she protests.

This is her trump card: If you don't let her do her homework, she won't graduate from high school. If she doesn't graduate, she won't leave home, and you'll never get to use your phone again in your life.[1]

---

1. So intrusive is the telephone for the father of a teenage daughter, I've included a special chapter on it.

With all these words gushing in an unstoppable flood from his daughter, one might suppose that the teenage years are a time for very close communication with her, a time when fathers and daughters sit together and lovingly reflect on what a great job he has done raising his children. Well, one would be wrong.

By the time a girl turns thirteen, she basically regards her dad as a sort of hybrid, no-limit ATM that not only dispenses cash but is supposed to drive her to the mall in order to spend it. Conversation is not necessary, and when the father attempts it, the daughter can immediately squelch it by turning up the radio. Daughters also wear headphones, which enable them to turn up the radio even in places where there's not supposed to be one!

This makes it very difficult for the father, who sometimes needs to extract information from his daughter.

"Did you delete my files from the computer?" you'll demand.

She'll stare at you blankly, as if waiting for a translation from the interpreter speaking into her headphones.

"Can you *hear* me?" you'll bellow.

She'll pull one of the implants from her ear, and you hear the jarring notes from the song "Don't Ever Listen to Your Father" coming from the tiny speaker. "I'm not deaf," she'll complain.

This is a good opportunity to point out no, she's not deaf, but if she continues to listen to music with the volume turned up, she will be. Daughters really appreciate hearing stuff like this from their fathers.

"Did you delete my computer files?"

"Dad, I can't fix all your computer problems for you," she'll sniff. Back go the headphones, and you idly wonder what would happen if you plugged them into the wall socket.

This is how conversations with your daughter *should* go:

"Did you delete my computer files?"

"No sir, I just backed them up to floppies. Here you go."

"Thanks."

"Say, Dad, can I buy—"

"No."

"Okay, thanks! Oh, I wanted to know if I can go with this boy I know to the—"

"No."

"You don't have to tell me twice! Can I wash your car for you, maybe put some gas into it with my own money, or is there some other set of chores you'd like me to do instead?"

Even though the above dialogue sounds perfectly realistic to a father, it won't ever happen unless your daughter is hypnotized.

Some Haunting Dialogue with My Daughter

Here's a real-life conversation between my older daughter and myself.

Daughter: Hello, Dad? I need you to come pick me and Heather up.

Father: (*Calmly*) *What*? Where the hell are you? You were supposed to be home four hours ago!

Daughter: Is Mom there?

Father: No, she is not here. Where are you?

Daughter: I'm at the movies with Heather.

Father: Who said you could go to the movies?

Daughter: Well, it's not like I could help it!

Father: You couldn't *help* going to the movies? Wait a minute, why do you need me to pick you up . . . you've got the car!

Daughter: That's what I am trying to tell you is not my fault!

Father: *What* isn't your fault?

Daughter: That I *had* to go to the movies! You never listen to me!

(This is, of course, an absurd accusation. I am listening to her so intently I'm in danger of getting a hernia in my eardrum. My blood pressure has risen and sent extra blood to my brain so I can process what she is saying—I can actually *feel* the pressure pounding on the walls of my skull. It is not a new sensation.)

Father: You said you *had* to go to the library.
Daughter: Well, right, but that was before the car died.
Father: It died.
Daughter: And I was like two blocks from the movie theater.
Father: So it has taken you all this time to walk to the movie theater?
Daughter: No, we saw a movie, duh.
Father: Can you please tell me what happened, and try to arrange the events in a coherent fashion?
Daughter: (*Heavy sigh*) Okay, I'll say it *again*. I was driving to the library and the car died. So I came to the movie theater and called Heather. Well actually, since you want me to be *coherent*, I called Amanda, but she and Brooke were going to get their picture taken at the mall for Brooke's birthday, which I would really, really like for my birthday, they give you like a complete makeover. Wendy did one with, like, a cowboy hat, which was so cute you wouldn't believe it.
Father: We obviously have different definitions of the word "coherent."

Daughter: Huh?

Father: Like, never mind. So you, like, called Heather.

Daughter: Why are you talking like that?

Father: Please proceed with the story of how you were forced to see a movie. I'm fascinated by that part.

Daughter: Right. Well, she said she could come but she couldn't drive, but that her mom could like drop her off. I said that would be okay because my dad would have to come pick me up anyway. I told her she can spend the night, is that okay?

Father: Wait a minute. *I'm* picking you up?

Daughter: Me and Heather.

Father: I mean, *why* do I have to pick you up? What's wrong with the car?

Daughter: I *told* you.

Father: No, you said it died. That's meaningless. What exactly is wrong with it?

Daughter: Well, I'm sorry you find me so meaning-less, but I had to walk all the way to the movie theater. You'd think you'd feel a little sorry about that.

Father: Would you please *just answer me*?

Daughter: Are you sure Mom's not there?

Father: Honey, in a few more seconds I'm going to pull this telephone off the wall and heave it out into the street. Just define for me, using the word "like" as many times as you feel is necessary, what it means to you when you say the car is now dead.

Daughter: Well, it acts like it might be out of gas.

Father: Oh? I thought I gave you money for gas.

Daughter: You did, but I spent it on the movie. Heather was broke.

Father: *What?*

Daughter: Well, what was I supposed to do, make her wait in the lobby? She is like my best friend in the whole world.

Father: Why do you think the car might be out of gas?

Daughter: See, the little light came on that says, "Check gauges."

Father: Yes?

Daughter: So I figured it meant there was something wrong with the gas gauge, because it was like way below empty, and I knew that couldn't be right because I had to go to the library.

Father: The "Check gauges" light comes on to alert you to the fact that one of your gauges is indicating a problem. Such as, for example, no fuel in the tank.

Daughter: Well, how was I supposed to know? That's really stupid.

Father: What do you mean, "How was I supposed to know?" Have you ever heard of an owner's manual?

Daughter: Oh, Dad, no one reads the owner's manual to a *car*. Skittles.

Father: I . . . what?

Daughter: Heather is buying candy and she asked what I wanted and I said Skittles. I wasn't talking to *you*.

Father: I thought you said Heather had no money.

Daughter: Right, for the *movie*.

Father: Okay. Okay. Do you have any money left?

Daughter: A little.

Father: Enough to put some gas in the car?

Daughter: I guess. If you pay me back.

The process of explaining to my daughter that she and Heather would have to walk to a gas station, get a gas can, fill it, and put enough fuel in the stricken automobile to get it going again took more conversation than I have the stamina to relate, particularly when every other sentence uttered by my daughter contained the words "not fair." (It was "not fair" that *she* had to pay for the gas because it was not her car. It was "not fair" that Heather couldn't spend the night. And it was "totally not fair" she would actually have to *walk*.)

"Don't we have road service?" she demanded, outraged.

He Says, She Says . . .

Though fathers and daughters speak the same language, they do not speak the same language. The following words and phrases indicate the gulf between the two, and may be helpful should you find it necessary to attempt communication with a teenager.

When the father says, "You aren't going anywhere until you clean up your room!" the daughter hears, "Close the door to your room so I can't see it and then go to the mall!"

When the father says, "I need to use the phone," the daughter hears meaningless chatter, because who would Dad be talking to on the phone anyway?

When the father says, "You can borrow the minivan tonight," the daughter hears, "You aren't going to be doing anything with your friends tonight, because if you did you'd have to be seen driving the minivan, and then you'd be excommunicated from every social group at school except Geeks on Wheels."

When the father says, "Turn off the TV," the daughter hears *nothing*.

When the father says, "Your room is a disaster area!" the daughter hears, "I've been snooping around in your room."

When the father says, "No, you absolutely may not go

to the party, you are grounded," the daughter hears, "Ask your mother."

When the father hears, "I'm done with my homework!" the daughter is saying, "Well, except for my math. And my history. Also biology. So tomorrow right before school I'll be running around screaming and slamming things and asking you to *please* retype my report, it's due today and I need to do my math!"

When the daughter says, "Everybody else is going!" what she means is, "Every other teenage daughter is telling her father that everybody else is going."

Challenging Authority— an Involuntary Reflex

As any good father knows, families are best organized into patriarchies. It's like a herd of deer peacefully grazing under the watchful eye of the magnificent buck, who issues commands with majestic wisdom, which the other, lesser deer are to obey unquestioningly and worshipfully.[2]

Unfortunately, teenage daughters often have trouble comprehending this elegant and ecological arrangement. They even want to *argue*, which in the real world would

2. *Bambi*, Walt Disney Co., August 1942.

lead to them being banished from the herd and sent off to live with goats or something.

When attempting to challenge the authority of their fathers, teenage daughters always use the same logic—which is to say, none. (In the teenage brain, the areas devoted to "logic" and "obeying father" have been disconnected, with all the electrical current routed through the "I already know everything so don't try to tell me anything" circuits.)

Here are some of the more common indications that your daughter may be attempting to communicate with you.

- *Foot stomp.* She raises her right foot and then drives it down hard onto a floor, like a horse solving a difficult math problem. Used to signal the father that whatever is being blurted is particularly valueless, and thus requires this extra bit of antagonism to make it *seem* like a valid point is being raised. The best response is to immediately shift topics, from her statement "I *have* to go, everybody will be there" to "What are you trying to do, cause the basement ceiling to crack? Do you know how much it costs to replaster the ceiling?" (This kind of stuff drives teenagers crazy.)

- *"Why not?"* Particularly talented teenagers deliver this cry with such a potent combination of outrage and incredulity that the father may momentarily question his sanity.

> **Teenager:** Can I take the car and spend the week-end in Las Vegas with Heather and two boys I met at a party one time?
> **Father:** What? No!
> **Teenager:** Why *not*?
> **Father:** (*Stunned*) I . . . I don't know, I just . . . um . . .

Don't let this happen to you! Remember, as a father you have a right to make capricious, arbitrary decisions. In fact, just to show her who is boss, you may sometimes need to pile on additional decrees, so that *she* questions *her* sanity.

> **Teenager:** Can I take the car and spend the week-end in Las Vegas with Heather?
> **Father:** No! You need to trim the dog's toenails and replaster the basement ceiling!
> **Teenager:** I . . . I just . . . um . . .

■ *"Everybody else is doing it!"* Teenagers are like salmon—one of them thinks it is a good idea to swim upstream, and the next thing you know, they're all doing it. Worse, once they get up to the top of the stream . . . well, you don't want to know what sort of activity they're engaged in up there. Just remember, the only reason we have baby salmon is that teenage salmon leave the safety of their parents' place in the ocean and start hanging out in rivers.

To the teenage mind, this salmon mentality is not only justified, it represents the *ideal* mode of behavior. The proper response to this ploy is to reply, "If everyone jumped off a cliff, I suppose you would, too." (I'm not sure *why* this is the proper response, it just comes with being a parent, springing unbidden to your lips. It may be embedded in our genes. Be careful, though, that you don't use this potent device on your daughter in front of *your* parents, who have learned a communication device of their own: *the ironic smile.*)

■ *"You are the meanest man who ever lived."* This is a high honor, conferred upon the father of a teenage daughter approximately once a week. Unfortunately, there are no trophies, and your teenager is unlikely to stick around while you deliver your acceptance speech. Take comfort, however, in knowing that when you hear these words, you have done well, my friend.

■ *"The minute I turn eighteen I am moving out of here."* Alas, although you can get this statement in writing, have it notarized, blessed by the church, and file it with the U.S. Patent Office, when the time comes, they don't leave.

Conclusion

Clearly, conversing with a teenager can be one of the most valueless experiences you'll have as a parent. Yet you'll react to this lack of return on your investment by putting more and more time and effort into the process—I can't explain why this is. Why are you talking to them at all? Shouldn't you just write down what you want them to do, maybe send them an e-mail or something, and have that be the end of it? Why ask your teenage daughter a question like, "Where do you think you're going with my car keys?" when you *know* you aren't going to like the answer?

Remember, you didn't create this communication gap. There was a time when they listened to your voice, paying rapt attention to your every word. Admittedly, they were only eight months old, but nobody asked your permission to change, did they? Aren't there still foreign countries, like, I don't know, Nebraska maybe, where the family gathers around every evening to listen appreciatively to what Dad has to say? If there are not, there ought to be. You've got a lot of important stuff to talk about: you're the father.

The Relationship
(or Lack Thereof)
Between
Allowance
and Chores

They Live Rent Free, They Drive Your Car, You Provide Them with Food, Clothing, and Gasoline—So It's Only Fair That If You Want Them to Help Out Around the House, You Should Pay Them, Right?

Money is to teenage girls what oxygen is to a house fire. In a house fire, however, the home owner isn't expected to rush in with oxygen tanks whenever it appears the flames might be losing some of their strength. The home owner is, however, expected to rush in and solve all of his teenage daughters' cash flow problems. He's supposed to generate the cash, then flow it to his daughters.

The main vehicle for this flow is the allowance. The allowance is a particularly incendiary issue for fathers, as it stems from the root word "allow." Fathers do not like to "allow" when it comes to teenage daughters—it goes against their every impulse.

Teenagers really don't care for the concept of allowance either, because it usually is not sufficient in either amount or frequency to enable your daughter to live like Ivana Trump. This often forces a bizarre situation where the teenage daughter needs an "advance" against a future allowance—meaning, essentially, that the father winds up owing money to himself.

At my house, obtaining an advance on allowance requires attending a lecture series on Managing Your Money and constructing a petition that explains why a cash advance is necessary in order to meet a Life-Threatening Emergency. The whole process is more difficult than being accepted to dental school, but it seems worth the effort to my older daughter, who clearly feels it is her responsibility to ensure the continued survival of the American clothing industry.

Daughter: I need an advance on my allowance.

Reasonable Father: What? I just paid you your allowance yesterday.

Daughter: Right, but I had to repay Mom for money she loaned me so I could pay you back so you'd pay me my allowance!

Reasonable Father: (*After a minute*) Huh?

Daughter: Could I please just borrow an advance?

Reasonable Father: For what year? You already owe into early 2013.

Daughter: Well, if you'd give me a raise in my allowance, maybe I could pay you back faster!

Reasonable Father: Why do you need another advance? And please don't tell me it's to buy more clothing.

Daughter: But Dad, it's an *annual sale*. That means it only happens like once a year!

Reasonable Father: I know what "annual" means. Why do you want to go shopping? Did you find an area in your room that isn't properly buried in dirty clothes?

Daughter: (*Heavy sigh*)

Reasonable Father: How come your sister never asks me for money? Could it be she's displaying fiscal responsibility?

Daughter: Like, I'm sure I'd ever dress the way she does. Everything she has is hand-me-downs.

Reasonable Father: From you! They're clothes *you* handed down!

Daughter: Exactly.

Reasonable Father: Then, no. The answer is no.

Daughter: Fine. I'll ask Mom.

Not that "fiscal responsibility" actually describes my younger daughter's spending. Her room is festooned with scented candles, lithographs, stained-glass animals, and other *objets de teen* that represent a wholesale waste of money. Wind chimes hang like stalactites, merrily smacking me on the forehead whenever I enter her room to interrupt what appears to be a séance in progress.

Reasonable Father: Why do you need all this stuff? Are you building your inventory for a garage sale?

Younger Daughter: (*Looks away*)

Reasonable Father: Well, it's your money. [Which isn't exactly true. It's *my* money, which my wife and I have earned, only to have our younger daughter use it to turn her room into the set for the Home Shopping Network.] I just wish you understood that the value of a dollar isn't what you can buy with it, it's what you have to do to *earn* it.

Younger Daughter: (*A groan that is so exaggerated it has to be fake*)

Reasonable Father: That's why it doesn't make any sense to pay allowance unless you're working for it!

A Built-In Labor Force

Like most fathers, I support the view that children should earn their allowances by doing work around the house. "Why did we have them, if not as a source of cheap labor?" I have lamented to my wife. This is an unfortunate choice of words, since she immediately reminds me that only one of us did any "labor" to have them. I don't know why she keeps bringing this up.

Anyway, in my opinion cheap labor is similar to cheap jewelry in both quality and appearance, because when it comes to doing their chores, my children seem to believe it makes more sense to put their efforts into making it *look* like they're working than to actually accomplish the tasks. More than once I've been fooled by the sound of the vacuum into believing that my children are helping me with the housework, but when I take a break during halftime and wander in to cheer them on, I find the vacuum running unattended in the family room while a daughter talks on the telephone in another part of the house. If I send one of them in to clean up the bathroom, the satisfactory noise of water running to scrub out the tub evolves into what sounds suspiciously like the start of a four-hour bath.

Probably the root of the problem lies in the ludicrous teenage belief that they are somehow independent of their fathers. I don't know where they get this idea, but they seem to feel that they are capable of picking their own chores and not having their father do so for them. I know, it's laughable—but I really do think this is how they see the world. Imagine what they would come up with if you did allow this chaotic system to be implemented!

Legitimate Chores According to Teenage Girls

CHORE	EXPLANATION
Check the television for reruns of favorite television shows.	Well, before you get started working, you need to have the television going, or else what will you do for distraction?
Turn up the radio.	This is my favorite song! And no, it doesn't bother me that the television is also on—if it bothers *you*, why don't you leave?
Call a friend on the telephone.	Well, it's not like my life stops just because I'm doing chores. And it's not my fault that the cord doesn't reach very far. Why don't you buy a cordless phone?
Get out the ice cream.	All these chores are making me hungry! And no, I'm not going to put everything away when I'm finished. That's not my job.

Assigning Chores

For some reason, teenagers regard every task assigned them as some sort of temporary aberration—tolerated, perhaps, but certainly not to be repeated. This means that nearly every weekend the father must convene a special family meeting to discuss the assignment of family chores. It's as if the Founding Fathers, after holding the Constitutional Convention and drafting the law of the land, decided it was so much fun they should do it once a month.

To tell you the truth, a family meeting is actually more difficult to assemble than a Constitutional Convention, because your children quickly figure out what is going on and bolt from the house the moment you tell them you wish to speak to them. Lasso one and troop her into the living room, and she'll disappear while you're hunting down the others. Try to turn on the TV to anchor your child in place and you'll wind up wasting a half hour watching a rerun of *Baywatch*. The only technique I've found useful is to catch them lounging around the table on a Saturday like the Rockefellers having breakfast, insouciantly waiting for the maid to clean up the mess they've made preparing their Cocoa Puffs. Once we've gathered together, here's how my family meetings proceed.

> **Father:** All right, let's talk about the weekend chores we're going to do today.
> **Older Daughter:** I already did my chores!
> **Son:** Yeah, me too.

Father: These are special weekend chores, not your daily chores, and no, neither of you did those anyway.

Older Daughter: Well, I couldn't scrub the bathroom because (*points to younger daughter*) she was in there for like four hours taking a bath.

Younger Daughter: (*Rolls eyes*) You are such a liar.

Father: That doesn't matter; we have special weekend chores to discuss.

Older Daughter: I don't think she should be allowed to call me a liar.

Father: Don't call your sister a liar.

Younger Daughter: So when she lies, what should I call her? A non–truth teller that rhymes with the word "itch"?

Older Daughter: Did you just hear what she called me?

Son: Can I go ride my bike?

Father: No, sit down. Look, stop it, you two.

Younger Daughter: Us two? She started it.

Older Daughter: No, you started it.

Younger Daughter: No, you.

Older Daughter: No, you.

Father: Stop it! (*Deep breath*) Okay, let's go through the list of chores. The first one on the list is to sweep the garage.

Son: That's not my job!

Father: I didn't say it was your job.

Older Daughter: Why does he get to get away with doing nothing?

Father: He's not doing nothing.

Son: I'm not?

Father: No! I mean, yes you are. I'll get to you in a minute, son. We're on the first chore.

Son: It's okay, I don't want to do nothing.

Younger Daughter: Can I please just leave? This whole thing is disgusting.

Father: Nobody is leaving. Sit down.

Younger Daughter: (*Mutters something*)

Father: What did you say?

Younger Daughter: Nothing.

Older Daughter: She said this is a complete waste of time.

Father: Okay, look. You might as well clear your calendar, because we're doing chores today.

Older Daughter: She calls you dirty words all the time, Dad.

Younger Daughter: I do not!

Older Daughter: Do too.

Younger Daughter: Do not!

Older Daughter: Do too.

Younger Daughter: I'm not wasting my time talking to you. You have the brain of a rodent.

Older Daughter: You have the brain of a slug.

Younger Daughter: You have the brain of a bacterium.

Older Daughter: If a . . . Well, you have no brain at all.

Younger Daughter: You have no brain minus two.

Son: Dad?

Father: Yes, son?

Son: Could we go to the monster truck show this weekend?

Father: Let's just stay focused for a minute here. Now, the first job on the list is the garage.

Older Daughter: I cleaned it last week. It is somebody else's turn.

Father: No, you didn't clean it last week, because it has something like thirty days' worth of dirt built up in there.

Older Daughter: Well, you never said anything about dirt.

Father: I said to clean the garage. What did you think I was talking about?

Older Daughter: Well, it's not my fault. There's so much junk in there, I couldn't even get *at* the dirt!

Father: Cleaning it means putting the junk away.

Older Daughter: That's not fair!

Younger Daughter: I detest being with you people.

Older Daughter: I don't think she should be allowed to say that.

Father: Son? Where are you going?

Son: Huh?

Father: Please sit down until we are finished.

Younger Daughter: (*Disgusted sigh*)

Father: So that's settled, you're doing the garage.

Older Daughter: I do all the work around here! (*Stomps out, slams bedroom door*)

Father: Come back here!

Son: Can I go ride my bike now, Dad?

A Ten-Step Plan for Getting Your Teenagers to Do Their Chores

Step One. Stand between them and the television and clap your hands together sharply, announcing, "It is time to do your chores!" in a thundering voice, like God telling Adam and Eve that they are evicted from the Garden of Eden. Do not expect any reaction—they've spent several years mastering the expression of lassitude on their faces, and they won't even blink as you rattle the house with your paternal authority. This is just the opening salvo, exercised as much to get *you* pumped up as to have any impact on them. A caution: whatever you do, *don't look into their eyes*. The dearth of ambition you will see there is so acute it can suck the vitality right out of you and cause you to fall stricken to the couch, spending the rest of the day watching cartoons with your children.

Step Two. Turn off the television. It may take you several minutes to locate the remote control—be advised that I have looked it up in the owner's manual and determined that a lot of TV sets can be shut off via a button on their front panel. Familiarize yourself with this procedure ahead of time so you don't lose momentum.

When the television shuts down your teenagers will involuntarily flinch as their brains, cut off from life support, attempt to function on their own. It's not a pleasant sight. Be strong.

Step Three. In a loud, clear voice, shout the word "now" several times, repeatedly clapping your hands. Gradually, they will come to realize you are speaking—at least, they will tear their eyes away from the blank TV screen (in an effort as physically difficult as pulling up carpet) and look at you, blinking slightly as your hands come together. It's a rewarding moment, sort of like a doctor watching a patient emerge from a coma, but don't be fooled: their work-immunity response hasn't yet rushed to their bodies' defenses.

Step Four. They now recognize who you are. "Time to do chores!" you bellow. They look from the television to you and then back, processing what is happening, a look of panic crossing their faces. You are asking them to *work.* For a moment—just for a moment—they are struck numb with dread as they contemplate that they might actually be forced into such a repulsive action.

Step Five. "Now!" you tell them again, but you can see that something has changed: a certain resolve is creeping into their expressions, giving them a sullen strength. Prepare yourself. I'd rather reach into a bag full of wet cats than argue with a teenager.

Step Six. The outrage will pour from them in a torrent of noise and heat, sort of like the backwash from a jet engine. Whatever you do, don't listen to their protests. Through some special mechanism that scientists haven't fully explained (because, in their words, "Our lab rats don't argue with us"), for every response you make to a teenager's objections, two more will take their place. Worse, your logic circuits will suffer irreparable harm under the assault, causing you to spend the rest of the day wandering around muttering better comebacks to yourself. It doesn't really matter if you're unfair, if your children have critical social engagements scheduled for the mall, if they suddenly remembered they must tend to studying that they forgot about when you asked them on Friday if they had any homework, if you are mean and unreasonable and they never want to talk to you again: *you want them to do their chores.* Stick to this, lash yourself to it with a rope, close your eyes and face the shrieking storm, and keep repeating, "Do your chores now."

Step Seven. There will be a lull as your teenagers suddenly realize you are not to be dissuaded by illogic. Having failed to derail you with sheer vehemence, they decide to shift tactics toward deceit. You'll notice their eyes dart from side to side as they contemplate their escape. "All right," they'll snarl, cleverly acting as if it is costing them to give in. They know that a humble capitulation would rouse your suspicions—they're teenagers, they aren't supposed to do anything you say without at least token rebellion.

Step Eight. Time to announce what your children call your "beanos." "There will be no sleepovers," you intone, "until your chores are done. There will be no using the car, no talking on the telephone"—they gasp sharply—"and no friends coming over to visit even if it is an emergency because Burke and Heather broke up again. There will be no joy or laughter until your chores are done." Keep piling these on until they actually rise from the couch. Watch carefully how they move. If their shoulders are sloped under the weight of the world, and if their trudge is heavy with the pull of gravity set to several times its usual level, they are actually planning to do their chores. If there is some spring to their step, they are up to something. Usually, they are headed to the kitchen—you wouldn't deny the condemned a last meal before they get started, right? They need energy to work, right?

Step Nine. Seal off their escape routes. Pull some granola bars from your pocket. "If you get hungry, eat these," tell them. "If the phone rings, I'll answer it. If Heather comes over sobbing, I'll comfort her and tell her Burke's a jerk. I'll pick out the music to listen to. The clothes you are wearing are fine. You do not need to talk to your mother." With each announcement they will cringe: it is absolutely abhorrent to the teenage mentality to suppose that their parents know what they are thinking.

Step Ten. A teenager, once sent off to do work, will quickly suffer a complete dissipation of energy. There are glaciers that move faster than a teenage daughter doing her chores. Follow them around as they tend to their chores, urging them on with additional beanos. It's exhausting work for a father, though it does have one benefit: if your wife hands you a list of your own chores, you can explain to her that you can't get to them. You're too busy!

Conclusion

The teenage years represent a formative period in which your daughter goes from wasting money on childish things to learning how to waste money like an adult. Your job is to fund this process.

If you don't pay your daughters an allowance, they won't do their chores. If you do pay them, they won't do their chores, but at least you won't have to deal with continual requests to open your wallet for every purchase your children feel they must make. For the sake of a little peace and quiet, then, I recommend you go ahead and set up a regular money transfer, futilely identifying the chores they must do in order to be paid their allowance. (This is a pretty easy task. Just take the list your wife gave you and hand it to your children.)

The amount of allowance varies from family to family. Generally, the daughter desires an amount to cover her basic spending needs for the week—in other words, the family's entire gross adjusted income. Since only an OPEC country can supply a teenage girl with all the money she wants, your best move is to pick an amount that represents the child's contribution to the family, and then add $5, for a total of $5.

Your daughter will have a rather strong opinion on what she should be paid, but she doesn't get a vote. It's your decision and yours alone: you're the father.

The
Telephone

No More Important to a Teenager Than, Say, Oxygen

Teenagers are the only animals on the planet shown to have a nervous system that is (*a*) external to their bodies and (*b*) built by the telephone company.

When the telephone rings inside the house, it stimulates the special hyperadrenal glands that dominate a teenage girl's brain, sending anxious thoughts through her mind. *Who could it be? It must be important or they wouldn't be calling! I have to answer the phone!!!*

The otherwise largely unused teenage brain unites in a single, powerful impulse, propelling the daughter forward faster than a cheetah pursuing an antelope. If there is a teenage sister in the room, the phone signals the start of the teenage Olympics, with a combined event of the ten-yard dash and synchronized lamp destruction. Innocent lives are risked in the rush to answer the phone first.

Fathers believe it reasonable to pick up the telephone themselves if they are nearby. After all, the phone bill is paid by the parents, the home in which the instrument resides is owned by the parents, and sometimes the call is even for the parents.

Upon raising the instrument to the ear, the father will hear a hair-raising shriek, as if the person on the other end of the line is being electrocuted. "I've GOT it!" the daughter will be yelling. Holding the phone at arm's length to minimize damage to the eardrum, the father can more clearly identify the outraged cry of a teenager who has just been mortified that her father dared to speak the word "hello" into the phone, thus revealing to the caller that she lives in a home with parents and not rock stars.

"I *said* I got it! I got it!" she'll wail.

There are a number of ways a father can respond in this situation, all of them causing significant humiliation to the teenage daughter.

ACTION	TEENAGE HUMILIATION SCALE	ADULT HUMILIATION EQUIVALENT
Hang up the telephone without comment.	This is a solid 4 on the humiliation scale: the click on the line serves as proof you exist.	A 4 is the equivalent of giving a sales presentation with your fly unzipped—not life altering, but clearly an embarrassment you'd just as soon forget about.

ACTION	TEENAGE HUMILIATION SCALE	ADULT HUMILIATION EQUIVALENT
Pleasantly say, "Okay," and hang up.	A 6. Your tone implies you have a friendly relationship with your daughter. This is, of course, ludicrous, but the teenager on the other end of the line doesn't know this.	You're back in high school and as you hurry to class you realize you are clad only in a pair of underpants.
Say, "I need to use the telephone," and hang up.	Well, you've committed an 8 here. Implying you have the right to the telephone, that it is not the sole property of your daughter, puts her in a position of dependence so abhorrent to a teenager she is not likely to speak to you for several days.	Asking a woman to marry you and having her unable to reply because she is laughing so hard.
Asking, "Who is calling, please?"	There it is, a 10. You have broken a taboo so strong that you may never be forgiven. You have no right to this information, and just asking for it is a sin for which there is no forgiveness.	Taking the oath of office for president of the United States while clad only in your underwear and having the chief justice unable to speak because he is laughing so hard.

When teenage daughters speak on the telephone, they use a form of language totally baffling to a father, a steady deluge of words with no pause for breathing or even listening. Are both parties speaking simultaneously? It's very fortunate that the telephone bill is based on a flat rate and is not per word, or no parent could ever afford to have phone service in the house. The torrent begins the moment a teenager walks in the door from school, the instrument ringing out in joyous recognition of its best friend's return. Usually the person calling is the girl your daughter was just sitting *next to on the school bus*, and the conversation, if you can call it that, continues unabated for the rest of the evening.

A Week in the Life of a Teenage Telephone

I am convinced that if the FBI ever wiretapped my home in a criminal investigation, they would soon open fire on the place just to get my daughters off the telephone. Were they to try to log the substance of the blizzard of conversation, here's how it might look.

Monday: *Crisis.* Heather and Burke broke up.

Tuesday: *Crisis.* Heather says she will never get back together with Burke again. They've been dating forever, since before October. Ohmygod, Lindsey wants to go out with Burke.

Wednesday: *Crisis.* Heather found out that Lindsey wrote a note to Burke and gave it to Emily, so now Heather hates Emily. Lindsey says she's just friends with Burke—oh yeah right, Lindsey.

Thursday: *Crisis.* Now that Heather and Burke are back together they aren't talking to Lindsey or Emily. So Emily has invited Katie to her party on Friday, and you know Heather hates Katie because she used to go out with Burke, so now Heather *isn't going to the party.* This is like the worst thing that could possibly happen in my life.

Friday: *Crisis.* Heather and Burke had a big fight because he wants to go to the party even if Katie is there. Are they going to break up?

Saturday: *Crisis.* Heather and Burke broke up! Emily disinvited Katie because it was Katie's fault that Heather and Burke broke up, since Katie was planning to come to the party, so now Emily and Heather are friends again, thank God, because they are like my two best friends in the world except for Amanda, who is like my very best friend after Heather. Lindsey says she is sorry she wrote the note and wants to help Burke and Heather get back together—oh yeah right, Lindsey.

Sunday: *Crisis.* Heather and Burke didn't really break up, they just *said* they did to prove how two-faced Lindsey is. Now Lindsey says we have to choose who we're friends with, her or Heather. Well like I'm sure I'm going to pick *Lindsey.*

(*Sunday: Father calls the telephone company and asks to have his service disconnected.*)

Why Eavesdropping Is Not a Good Idea

After a certain amount of exposure, fathers usually become completely numb to their daughters' telephone conversations and are able to ignore them even when they are taking place right in front of them. This is a defensive response, initiated by the paternal nervous system to prevent stress-induced hypertension. Without this natural reflex, fathers might find themselves listening in to one side of the conversation—a particularly unsettling experience.

Older Daughter: Hi, Heather!
(*You're pretty sure you know which one is Heather.*)
Older Daughter: Oh *no.* What happened?

(The distress in your daughter's voice is palpable, and you lower your newspaper slightly. If Heather and Burke are breaking up again, you may have to kill yourself. The last time this happened, four teenage girls showed up in a crisis-mismanagement response team, sobbing in a manner for which the word "hysterical" was invented.)

Older Daughter: He did *what?*

(He did*? This is not good. You don't want any he doing any what to any body even remotely associated with your daughter. You drop your paper and lean forward to listen, straining like a man passing a gallstone.)*

Older Daughter: Ohmygod, Heather. Where were you?

(Where were you*? Where were your parents, Heather? Why didn't you have the sense to stay broken up one of the last dozen or so times you and Burke swore your relationship was as dissolved as the U.S.S.R.?)*

Older Daughter: Then what happened?

(There's more? Isn't this bad enough?)

Older Daughter: Well, don't worry. I've done that.

(Wait a minute. You have? How could this be? What do you mean, don't worry? *Worry is exactly what is*

*called for in this situation! It was for times like this
that God invented worry in the first place!)*

Older Daughter: Well, don't tell him, then.

*(Don't tell who? Heather's father? They're keeping
secrets from their fathers? That's it, your daughter
is forbidden to leave the house without a paternal
escort. You don't want her even talking to boys until
she's married.)*

Older Daughter: Okay! Well, I'm glad you called.

*(You're not. Your skin feels like it was left out in
the rain and all the blood has rushed from your
head and gone elsewhere, perhaps to New Jersey.
You wonder if you should telephone Heather's dad
and tell him, man-to-man, father-to-father, exactly
what's going on. Except, well, you don't really know.
And that's the worst part of all of this.)*

The Teenage Daughter as Secretary

Teenagers frankly disbelieve their parents have important
phone calls. To have an important telephone call implies
an important life, a clearly ludicrous concept when applied
to a teenage daughter's father. Thus, there is never any
compelling reason to write down any information when

someone manages to pierce through the nearly impene-
trable shield of busy signals your daughters have erected
around the family's phone system and asks to speak to a
parent—messages are conveyed orally, if at all, and usually
in the following format.

Teenage Daughter: Dad, some guy called.

Father: Who?

Teenage Daughter: I don't know, but he said it was
important.

Father: Was it a business call, or a personal call?

Teenage Daughter: I don't know.

Father: Was it a relative?

Teenage Daughter: No, I said it was some guy, duh.
He called you "Mr. Cameron."

Father: So it was probably a business call.

Teenage Daughter: Whatever.

Father: Did he leave a phone number?

Teenage Daughter: Yes, but I didn't write it down.

Father: Why not?

Teenage Daughter: Don't yell at me.

Father: I'm not . . . Look, don't you think it is reasonable that when someone calls for me, you write down
his telephone number, and maybe the reason for his
call?

Teenage Daughter: Well, I didn't have time to be reasonable, I had to call Heather. It was an emergency.

Father: (*Not wanting to hear about Heather's emergency*) Okay. This guy who called, did he say anything at all?

Teenage Daughter: Yeah, something about 1998.

Father: Nineteen ninety-eight?

Teenage Daughter: Yeah.

Father: Some guy called and said something about the year 1998.

Teenage Daughter: That's it!

Father: No, that is not "it." What about the year 1998? Was he just calling to reminisce?

Teenage Daughter: I don't know, it was complicated. He's from a service.

Father: A service.

Teenage Daughter: Whatever.

Father: A service station?

Teenage Daughter: Sure.

Father: A man called from a gas station to talk about 1998.

Teenage Daughter: I can't believe you are making such a big deal out of this.

Father: A service . . . Wait a minute, do you mean the *Internal Revenue Service*?

Teenage Daughter: I guess so. That could have been it.

Father: You guess so? Someone calls from the IRS and says he wants to talk to me about the tax year 1998, and you didn't even think to take a message? I'm being audited by the Internal Revenue Service, and you didn't even bother to get the man's name?

Teenage Daughter: Well, why do I have to take a message? You obviously already know all about it!

A Friendly Letter from the Phone Company

Dear Mr. Cameron:

Congratulations on your second telephone line! Here are some hints on how to make the most effective use of your new services.

1. A Second Line. With the introduction of your second line, now both of your daughters will be able to talk on the phone at the same time, reducing the shrieking that normally ensues when one of them is chatting and the other one wants to make a call. Of course, your second line will do nothing to improve your *personal* access to a telephone. Did you think it would?

2. Conference Calling. Each of your daughters now has the capability of calling two friends and talking to them at the same time. This will drastically improve their communications, because, for example, normally when Heather and Burke break up, your oldest has to contact each of her girlfriends separately, which can take all night. And consider this. With your two lines, at any given time six teenage girls could be conversing at once. And if your daughters' friends have conference calling (and most of them do), why, the whole volleyball team could talk at once. The possibilities are limitless. You, however, will not enjoy any more use of the phone than was the case before—you didn't think you would, did you?

3. MSBS (Multiple Simultaneous Busy Signals). When people attempt to reach you, they will now have two numbers to try—both of which will respond with a busy signal. You didn't think having two lines would result in people being able to contact you, did you? We advise that you sign up for Call Waiting. With Call Waiting, continual clicking will punctuate every sentence, until conversation becomes impossible. With *Multiple* Call Waiting, your daughters' calls will stack up like jets circling

O'Hare on a snowy day. None of these features will result in people being able to contact *you*—you didn't think they would, did you?

4. An Added Benefit. When neither of your daughters is home, you'll find that both lines will be ringing simultaneously and continuously. This will enable you to sharpen your message-taking skills, a valuable commodity in today's job market. The phone will almost never be for you, unless it is someone wanting to sell you long distance services. (Pretty ironic, don't you think?)

As a final gesture of our thanks, we are enclosing a map that clearly indicates where you will be able to find a pay phone, which is the only way you are going to be able to make a telephone call.

Sincerely,

The Phone Company

There Are No Remedies

A reasonable father might decide that his house is better off without a telephone altogether. After all, didn't the human race survive for many centuries without this infernal device? (Though I will note that none of the cave drawings uncovered to date depict a teenage girl. Perhaps they didn't *have* teenagers back then, which is why they didn't need a telephone.)

Disconnect your phone service, though, and you're likely to get a visit from Human Services, following up on the report your daughters made at school that their father was torturing them. (I don't think that a jury would convict on this charge, however—in fact, if the court empanels any parents, they would be more likely to burst out in applause.)

I've checked with the telephone company about putting a pay phone in the house, but they refused to consider it. Apparently they tried this once and a frantic teenager, unable to find any change in the house, was forced to break into her father's coin collection in order to be able to find out what everyone else was wearing to the party. The phone company doesn't want any more legal liability than it already has.

Conclusion

It would be easier to understand why your teenage daughters appear to have a telephone surgically attached to the sides of their faces if they were discussing anything of real importance. If you monitor what they are saying (not recommended for long periods of time) you'll quickly determine that what they're talking about with such urgency (*a*) makes no sense, (*b*) is the same stuff they were talking about yesterday, last week, and last month, and (*c*) revolves around who said what to whom about what she was wearing, and never around academic subjects or what to get Dad for Father's Day. This means whatever your daughter needs to talk about cannot really matter, and she should hang up the phone—though when you make this declaration, you're likely to be overruled by your wife, who pretends she isn't irritated by the whole situation.

"They're her friends, dear," she'll say to you patiently. "You can't deny her access to her friends."

Well, who says you can't? Of course you can: you're the father!

Field
Observations

A Highly Scientific Study of Teenagers in Their Natural Habitat: The Mall

R esearching this book, I spent many hours among teenagers, observing their habits, learning their language, and preventing their mating rituals. Over time, I've come to appreciate them for what they are: a completely alien species competing with *Homo sapiens* for scarce planetary resources.

When they are at home, teenagers spend most of their time in their bedrooms, where they burrow under mounds of dirty clothes and hibernate until noon. It's frankly a whole lot easier for fathers if they don't ever enter their teenagers' lairs, though it *is* a good place to go if you're curious where all the dishes in the house have disappeared to. Teenage girls don't appear to accomplish anything in their rooms. Mostly, they lie on their beds and exercise what they consider to be their constitutional rights of sloth, apathy, and the pursuit of torpor.

Around the age of thirteen, teenage daughters suddenly develop an urge to spend every weekend at the local mall. Fathers have every right to be suspicious of such impulses—when your daughter is thirteen, you should regard every motive as completely suspect. A reasonable father will deny permission to go—you don't even need to think about it.

"What's *wrong* with going to the mall?" everyone in the family will want to know. Be careful of this question: it's a trap. There's nothing wrong with the mall except that at Christmastime it drains your credit lines. What's wrong is that your daughter wants to go there. As a father, that's all you need to know.

Code of Conduct
for Driving Your Teenage
Daughter to the Mall

A young teenage girl depends on her parents to drive her to the mall. This seems like a terrible burden, but if you think you can escape chauffeur duty, you are sadly mistaken: deny her a ride and the next weekend a tattooed sixteen-year-old boy will swing a loud, dark-windowed automobile into your driveway and your daughter will flash out the front door so quickly you will barely have time to call 911. She'll be missing all day without so much as a phone call, and won't return until you've already got the search party organized. The next time she wants to go, you'll *beg* her to let you drive. And she'll agree, but there are some rules you need to know.

Okay, when we get to the mall, sort of slide down in your seat so that none of my friends will see you. Do *not* drive right up to the front door!!! Drop me off about twenty yards back, behind the recycle bin. Do not ever, ever ask me if I know the kids who are standing out in front smoking cigarettes. Do not ask me who I am meeting. Do not ask me how long I will be there. Do not talk to me.

Just in case some of my friends are around, I will jump out of the car and slam the door as if I am really angry at you. Do not ever, *ever*, roll down the window and shout something after me. Even though I will pretend I can't hear you, my friends might hear you. I don't want them to think you and I talk to each other. Oh and don't *ever* say, "You're welcome," like you're making some sort of brilliant point because I didn't say thank you.

If you're going to give me money please do so before we get to the mall. I would be like *so* embarrassed if people thought I was getting money from my parents. I'll need about $10 for lunch. Also, there are some things I need that will cost $40. Plus you owe me back allowance.

Don't ever ask me to buy something for you at the mall, like I'm sure I would do that. I would be so embarrassed if I had to buy, like, a *screwdriver* or something with my friends right there. But don't come into the mall yourself to get it! Find a different place to go. I would be so embarrassed if I saw you there.

When it's time for you to come pick me up I'll call you. I do *not* want to get in some conversation! I'll just say, "I'm ready to be picked up," and that's it. Please don't ask, "Who is this?" It wasn't funny the first time. When you pull up, drive past the front door but do *not* wave at me! Pull over and park and I'll come by in a while. Just wait there for me and do *not* honk your horn. I know you're there! It is like so embarrassing for you to be sitting there honking like some big jerk.

When I'm ready I'll come out, and I'll walk over to the driver's side and tell you I want to drive. Do *not* make a big deal about the fact that I'm not even old enough for a learner's permit. When you say no I'll roll my eyes and make a disgusted face at my friends as I walk around to the passenger side and get in. I will slam the door and stare out the side window and be completely unresponsive. If you must talk to me, face straight ahead and try not to move your lips. Leave the area immediately.

Okay, on the way home, do not ask me who I saw, do not ask me what I did, do not ask me if I bought anything "special," do not ask to see what I bought, do not ask me if I had fun. I did not go to the mall to have "fun." I will talk to you, particularly if I am hungry and want to stop at the drive-thru, but please let's just keep the conversation to a minimum. I am like so disgusted to be talking to you. Do not ask me what happened to the money you gave me for lunch. If you saw me talking to a boy and you ask me about it I will never talk to you again for as long as I live, I swear.

When we get home I will go straight to my room and turn up the stereo. I need time to be alone. Please do not follow me—my room is my property. If I need something from you I will let you know. I hope we're not having something disgusting for dinner.

A Field Study of Teenagers

At considerable personal risk, I decided to investigate the lives of teenagers, going right into their midst—into the snake pit, if you will. It is sort of like when Jane Goodall went off to live with the gorillas, except I'll bet they never asked her for money or stole her shirts when she wasn't looking. I picked a Saturday when I knew the objects of my scrutiny would be gathered in large numbers—it was a bright, sunny day, which to a teenager is perfect weather for spending ten hours inside the mall.

To study teenagers, no elaborate camouflage is necessary—teenagers have very poor eyesight, recognizing only one another. An adult is completely invisible, unless you happen to run across your own daughter, who will frown and shake her head, humiliated that you are out in public where her friends might spot you. Attempt to approach her and she will whirl away, seizing a girlfriend's arm and racing into a store. If you pursue, they will seek refuge in the ladies' room.

Tribal Elders

In a building positively teeming with teenage life, at first it isn't evident that their social order is broken down into very specific groups. In fact, their directionless meanderings make it appear as if there is no organization whatsoever. One must remain very still, sitting on one of the benches the teens refer to as "geezer gazebos," to gain an understanding of these complex tribes.

Species: *Teenagis Narcissus*

The first group one notices is the older teenage girls. These are the queens of their order, survivors who have managed to return to the mall again and again despite their fathers' exasperated demands that they do something productive with their weekends. They generally travel in packs of three or more, and seem to congregate together based on commonality of eye makeup and breast size. They make extensive use of reflective surfaces to effect minute adjustments to their appearance. This group suffers at the hands of incompetent laundry workers, who can't seem to manage to clean their clothes without shrinking them until they are so tight their fathers have trouble breathing.

Though they reign over the mall, the older teenage girls seem somewhat lost, wandering in large circles. Rarely do they make any purchases from the stores—the whole point of their afternoon seems to be to prove that they are capable of walking and chewing gum at the same time. (Some also employ their fingers in the operation, stretching out thin strings of pink goo in front of their vacuous eyes.)

Species: *Teenagis Obnoxius*

Completely distracted by this group are the older teenage boys, who appear to have even less purpose to their lives. If the pack of boys is larger than three, one of them will walk backward out in front of the group, speaking loudly to the others like the leader of a marching band. They make as much noise as possible as they move through the building.

Unable to master the mechanics of a handshake, they continually slap at one another's hands, sometimes leaping in the air and whooping. They seem pretty convinced that everyone in the mall is watching them in fascinated admiration.

Unlike the girls, these boys have plenty of room in their clothing. In fact, I suspect that in a pinch, three or more of them could fit into a single pair of pants. None of them have figured out the intended use of the baseball cap—they wear them on the proper appendage, to be sure, but they cannot understand the purpose of the bill, and usually wear it facing to the rear. Those that have the bill pointing in the right direction have it so curled that it looks as if their faces are peering out from behind a rolled-up newspaper.

Though they are there primarily to interact with the mall queens, the boys spend most of their time avoiding eye contact. They slouch past a group of queens as if unaware of their existence, but the second they are past they turn as one to observe the girls as they retreat. Should one of the girls look back over her shoulder, the boys recoil as if shot.

The countless miles of aimless meandering seem to take a toll on both groups. The girls begin scuffing their feet, particularly when they are in the vicinity of a pack of boys, while the male teenagers adopt a gimpy gait that suggests juvenile arthritis.

Seemingly Random Encounters

From time to time, these older groups actually meet— a pained ritual that is fascinating to watch.

The contact is initiated by the queens, one of whom will flip her hair or pointedly turn her head as a group of males mournfully shuffles by. This will cause the boys to halt and huddle, consulting with one another in a manner that suggests pure panic. Gesturing wildly, the one who was singled out will make the case for pursuit, but the others appear dubious. There's often a lot of loud laughter, though from the tense expression on their faces, it's clear that there is little funny in this situation.

Often the ritual ends there, the boys drifting on,

unable to convince themselves they ever really had a chance. Sometimes, though, the pack will scurry to catch up to the queens, but do so in such a way as to be on the other side of the wide corridor as they pass. Apparently the boys believe they are invisible to the girls as they hustle past like football players running downfield. Then they circle around, seemingly coincidental in their approach, as they attempt to duplicate the contact of moments before. At this point, the girls are merciless, giving no sign they are even aware that the boys exist. The second pass ends in confusion, the boys mystified by this cool response when things went so well the first time.

With a little more resolve, however, there is a different outcome. The boys set out in pursuit of the girls, who deliberately slow their pace to allow themselves to be overtaken. The boys shove their hands in their pockets. The girls turn to offer a united front. The boys stare at their fronts. There's a moment of heightened suspense, broken when one of the males speaks. "Hi," he'll offer, looking away as if he couldn't care less if he gets a response. Glancing at one another, the girls acknowledge the greeting, and the introduction is complete.

One might suppose that, having successfully completed this ritual, the teenagers would proceed to some next step in the elaborate process. But this is where teenagers are perplexing to real people—for all the effort they've just expended, they don't actually accomplish anything. The now coed group attempts to effect cohesion as it moves en masse through the mall, but there are too many stresses at work. The boys, afflicted with nervous energy, want to prowl more quickly, and push and slap at one another maniacally, like the Three Stooges overdosing on caffeine. Proud of their acquisitions, they affect a curious strut— one can almost imagine them leaning over to peck at some birdseed on the ground. The queens bunch up, glancing at one another as they hold up the rear of this strange procession, carrying their shoulders back and chests forward to accentuate the most prominent differences between themselves and the males. I call this commingled gait the "strut and jut," and as a father, it's difficult to watch without becoming queasy.

The boys don't seem to want to talk to them, though they do continually glance over their shoulders at the girls to make sure they've impressed the females with their antics. Eventually, the titanic forces that brought them together wind up forcing them apart—the girls peel off and enter a store, waving hastily. The boys pretend they don't care, though as soon as the girls have vanished, their step slows and they become morose. Their sullen and desultory wandering continues lethargically until they become energized by the appearance of another group of queens.

Rarely, but occasionally, one of the boys will exchange contact information with one of the queens, a phone number handed over on a slip of paper. This is the point at which any reasonable father might feel compelled to leap up from the bench, reveal himself, and chase off the boy, but as a true scientist I forced myself to observe without interfering.

Naturally, I would have made an exception if it had been my own daughter.

Species: *Teenagis Liplockis*

At some point, a few of the older teenagers leave their gender-based herds and form couples. This can happen at virtually any time, though most fathers would prefer it not occur until their daughters have left the mall for the day.

Teenage couples at the mall often stroll around holding hands. They gaze at the store windows with eyes full of wonder, as if they are in the streets of Paris. Often, one of them will point out something to the other, a potted plant or a fountain, and they will marvel with large eyes at stuff that's been there the whole time.

Teenage couples contrive the most ridiculous reasons to bump into each other, occasioning a knowing grin and, worse, a quick kiss. The boy will stop and turn suddenly, which he would never do under any other circumstance, and there they are, colliding softly, apologizing with their lips in a most inappropriate public display of affection. The mall security guards are totally worthless in these situations, refusing to deploy pepper spray or even to let me borrow it for a few moments.

The New Initiates

Unlike most primitive species, teenagers mark the passage from childhood into fully unproductive mall citizens with no special ceremony or ritual. Initiation into the tribe consists of nothing more formal than being dropped off at the mall entrance by an anxious-looking parent. It's not even obvious that these youngsters are really teens, in the legal sense—some appear to be no older than eleven. Yet by their appearance, they are announcing to the world that, thirteen or not, they are ready to begin behaving like teenagers.

Species: *Teenagis Underdevelopis*

The younger girls make their appearance at the mall as if not sure they're allowed to be there. Unlike the queens, who stroll up and down with a certain swagger, these girls lean into one another, often to the point where it appears that a single misstep by one will send the entire group toppling like dominoes. Very often they are chewing on their necklaces, and they say "Ohmygod" to one another a *lot*. They are gawky and nervous, and visibly shrink when a more mature female struts past wearing a bra for which "push-up" seems inadequate—perhaps "torpedo" does better to capture the spirit of the thing.

Not fully understanding the true, entirely social purpose of the mall, younger teenage girls usually carry purchases with them, small bags containing trinkets that they've bought for reasons they can never explain to their fathers, who will often demand to know just how many mood rings a person needs.

These girls seem to be on a mission. They walk much more quickly than the older females of their species, and appear excited by the window displays. Very often they cluster around the telephones, probably calling one another. "I'm at the mall," one pictures them saying. "Where are you?"

"At the mall."

Where else would they be?

Younger teenage girls preen in public. Often a group of them will collapse on a bench and spend hours grooming one another, brushing and braiding hair and exchanging too much makeup.

Sometimes one of them will take a step back out of the group, move her arms in a synchronized motion, clap, and jump in the air. While this looks like some sort of plea for psychiatric help, it is actually a pseudo cheerleading move, though it is unclear if the girls performing these muted gymnastics are, in fact, cheerleaders. The queens *never* do this.

When a group of younger teenage girls passes a music shop and hears a popular tune, they will smile at one another and perform a brief dancing motion. No one knows why they do this. When a father asks what this odd behavior is all about, the teenage girl will deny ever doing it, with a vehemence more characteristic of murder suspects.

Species: *Teenagis Cluelessis*

Young teenage boys wander through the mall absolutely determined not to be trapped in a position where they might actually converse with a girl. They gawk at the queens, often losing track of where they are going and colliding with walls and security guards. They like to throw coins in the fountain and to lean over the railings on the top floor and attempt to peer down women's blouses. They demonstrate a complete lack of purpose to their lives.

These gawky, ill-formed creatures enjoy far more visibility with their female counterparts than do older boys with the queens. Giggling, waving, and staring, the newly formed teenage girls communicate a brazen welcome to the young males, who in turn seem utterly confused. Agitated by the attention, they are afflicted with a disturbed energy that sometimes sends them running away from the girls, laughing as if their flight is a hilarious joke.

Watching them, it's impossible to imagine that they will ever evolve into productive human beings.

Other Teen Species

The mall is like an ocean reef, teeming with life. Yet some teenagers eschew the environment that attracts so many of their peers, choosing instead to lurk outside the safety of the walls. Faced with a far different ecosystem than the teens who inhabit the interior, these subgroups have evolved into entirely separate classes of teenager, characterized by different and complex social customs.

Species: *Teenagis Sullen Rebellis*

The smokers camp right outside the front doors and blow pollution at everyone attempting access. They sit on the cement walls, dangling their feet, and affect perpetually surly expressions. Forced to survive in the unpredictable temperatures of outside air, they often wear leather and dark clothing, sunning themselves like cold-blooded reptiles. Some have shaved their heads, but only portions of them, as if they became fatigued after a while and could no longer wield the razor.

Species: *Teenagis Extremis*

Farther down the parking lot, hanging out by the loading ramps, are the skateboarders, boys who attempt to achieve bone fractures by riding rubber-wheeled devices down stairs and along steel railings. Given their muscular agility, one would be tempted to classify these odd teens as athletes, except the only possible name for the sport would be "self-destruction." How it can be fun to throw oneself facedown on the pavement is something only these fellows know. I sometimes think of them as the Lost Boys, completely oblivious to the fact that their cousins are inside the mall meeting girls and avoiding ambulances.

Species: *Teenagis Internal Combustis*

Out in the parking lot itself is another odd group: the car boys. Gathered around a row of shiny automobiles, they spend hours looking at engines, revving their motors, and blaring their stereos. They don't seem to grasp the fact that the automobile was invented for transportation. Often their cars sit low to the ground—anything in the road larger than a walnut would tear the mufflers right off the frames. At the other extreme, pickup trucks tower in the air, with suspension systems built out of extension ladders. No one can climb up into these vehicles without assistance from a stool, or maybe a pole vault.

Species: *Teenagis of Other Parentis*

Occasionally one will spot some completely normal-looking kids who are tossing a football back and forth in the grass. They not only are aware of adults, but will actually nod and smile as one passes. One gets the feeling that were one to ask, these kids would help load packages in the trunk of one's car. Girls sit in the sun and laugh with one another. These youngsters appear clean-cut and healthy, and must have wandered in from 1956.

Research Conclusions

When architects and construction engineers first envisioned shopping malls decades ago, they were probably focused on the immediate benefits of their creations—the destruction of downtown retail districts, traffic congestion, the creation of megachains with little product differentiation, and deforestation in the name of parking lots—and weren't contemplating the impact these places would have on the teenagers of future generations. As it turns out, had the malls not been constructed, the teenagers of today might have been forced to turn to productive activities to fill their weekends.

My wife often asks me what I have against our daughters spending the day at the mall. Teenagers, she postulates ridiculously, need some place to *go*. Well okay, I respond, they can *go* out into the yard and rake leaves or *go* into the garage and pick up the junk that's been blocking me from parking my car there since the early eighties. Why do they have to hang out where there are all sorts of dangers lurking, like boys and clothing sales?

It is a well-known fact that teenagers will move quickly to exploit any crack in the alliance between parents. To properly raise them, the mother and father must present a united front. It is therefore critical that fathers be firm in their opposition to weekend visits to the mall and not be dissuaded by mere logic.

Yes, it can get to be very unrewarding, being right all the time. But you must stick to your guns on this issue: That's your job. You're the father.

Crime and Punishment

When Old Methods of Discipline No Longer Work, You Must Use New Methods, Which Won't Work Either

O ne of the few pleasures associated with being the parent of a teenage daughter is devising ever more creative punishments for her. In the process, you will "ruin her life," which sounds like it might be a pretty ambitious goal but is actually pretty easy.

Father: You're not going anywhere until you do the dishes.

Daughter: You're ruining my life!

(No one ever asks what having a couple of teenage daughters has done to *your* life.)

What's perplexing about teenage girls is that they don't seem to grasp the connection between their behavior and the resulting punishment, even when your face turns purple and you pound on the kitchen table with your fist. Your daughter will commit the same violation over and over again, leading you to increase the severity of the consequence in a fruitless attempt to get her to *listen, would you please just listen?!*

Sorry.

Anyway, if a father isn't careful, this escalating cycle can lead to (*a*) an embolism and (*b*) overpunishment. Overpunishment occurs when the punishments you've handed out, when added together, wind up being *your* punishment. If you ground your daughter for more than a week or two in a row, for example, you'll find your nerves jangling on a scale somewhere between six cups of coffee and electroshock therapy. Take away her driving privileges and you'll wind up becoming Chauffeur for the Day. Oh, and you may think that preventing her from using the telephone is especially clever, but then you'll just have a steady stream of teenage girls flooding your house because of an "emergency."

A Reasonable Father's List of Prohibited Activities

A teenage girl is a work in progress, who must sample life's experiences in order to learn and grow. A father's job is to prevent this process for as long as possible. To do so, he must be very firm and specific in his list of prohibited activities, or his daughter will find a loophole. (I would pit teenage girls against the highest-paid attorneys in the country—when it comes to the nuances of the law, my daughters could make the justices of the Supreme Court *weep*.)

> **Father:** I thought I told you that you couldn't go out tonight.
>
> **Daughter:** I asked if I could go out with Brittany, and you said no. I went out with *Katie*.
>
> **Father:** (*Audible sound of brain exploding*)

Here is a very reasonable breakout of things that are on the Absolutely Not list for teenage daughters.

Motorcycles

Are you out of your mind? Do you have any idea how dangerous those things are? Let me put it to you this way: only a complete and utter idiot would get on the back of a machine whose sole protection against collisions with other objects is air. And stop showing me photographs of myself when I was your age riding *my* motorcycle—that's completely irrelevant.

Beating on Your Little Brother

Despite what you may think, your brother was not put on this earth so that you would have something to punch. I find his wailing irritating, so please desist. And let me try to clue you in on a little biology. Yes, right now his muscles are like limp spaghetti, but he is growing at a rate of a couple of inches and several pounds a year, whereas you've stopped growing everywhere but your mouth. Take a moment to calculate how much bigger he is at this age than you were, and you can see you have only about twelve months left before he can start hitting back with real effect. Do you really think he's going to forget all the poundings you've administered over the past several years? I don't. If I were you, I'd sue for peace *now*.

Parties

Since you've been so unreceptive to my perfectly reasonable request that I be allowed to go to all parties to which you are invited, it can only lead me to one conclusion: there's something going on there that you don't want me to see. I really don't care if "everybody else" will be there—in fact, that's a strong argument why you shouldn't go! It's what you do with the other kids that worries me.

Kissing

Your lips get enough strain talking on the telephone and don't need to be subjected to the stress of having some boy's mouth pressed against them. Furthermore, kissing has unpredictable effects on the male brain and often sends random signals to his hands. You need to keep your own germs in your own mouth and not share them with others. And if you really have that much free time with your lips, why don't you learn to play the bugle?

Tattoos

A tattoo is like having a miniature *Exxon Valdez* crash into your body, staining your skin forever. And have you ever noticed that when the newspapers carry descriptions of wanted criminals, they nearly always seem to have tattoos? You never read, "Günter Grass, 1999 winner of the Nobel Prize for literature, is described as five feet, ten inches tall, with a tattoo under his left eye of a carnivorous snake eating a rabbit."

Please do not furnish me with a list of friends whose parents have allowed tattoos to permanently sully their daughters' skins. To me, this is just proof that people are abusing their reproductive rights. And don't even bother to describe Heather's tattoo as "small and tasteful." The little dots of green mold that form on bread are "small." Does that make them "tasteful"?

You may not under any circumstances get a tattoo. That's my reasonable compromise on the issue.

Boys in Your Room

Are you crazy? I have been to your room and I know that somewhere underneath all those clothes there is a bed. When a boy sees a bed with a girl standing next to it, he always thinks it is a good idea to lie down. Until you have moved out of my house and turned thirty, you are to remain standing upright in the presence of all boys.

Boys Late at Night in the Living Room

When you turn out all the lights and sit down on the couch to watch a movie on TV with a boy, do you really think his attention will remain focused on the screen very long? Plus, our couch is small and I am often very uncomfortable squeezed in between you two.

Boys

When it comes right down to it, boys are an unnecessary accessory in your life right now. Their minds are drenched in a chemical called testosterone, which strips out rational thought, misappropriates blood flow, and causes irrational (and in my house, very dangerous) behavior. Surely you agree boys are awkward and unattractive, with hands that are too large and too exploratory. If you are curious, you can see boys on television, and I am sure they must have a Web site.

An Ounce of Prevention . . .

Often as I sit in my chair watching sports on TV, drinking beer, and eating potato chips, I reflect on how to best prevent my children from developing unhealthy vices. The tactics must be radically different for each daughter, taking into consideration the maddening diversity in their personalities.

Cigarette smoking, as an example, was never an issue with my oldest child, who would view any diminishment of her lung capacity as an impediment to dominance of her athletic rivals, but my younger daughter seems more vulnerable to peer pressure. Her vampire-looking friends sometimes reek of smoke when I step outside to explain that my daughter isn't home because I say she isn't.

When I came across an unopened pack of cigarettes in my younger daughter's desk drawer, I wasn't looking for trouble, just a blank floppy disk to back up a file before my computer decided to toss it out the Windows®, which has happened too often in the past. I stared at my find with a sense of dread and failure, realizing that I was going to have to try something other than a "straight talk" with my younger teenager, with whom I'd already had the following conversation.

Father: I want to talk to you about smoking.

Daughter: (*Eye rolling and head shaking*)

Father: What? Don't shake your head, I'm talking to you.

Daughter: (*Head stops shaking, eyes stare right through me as if she has X-ray vision*)

Father: (*Controlling breath*) Smoking is dangerous. It causes cancer and increases the danger of stroke. It causes death, which I feel is something to be avoided if possible.

Daughter: (*Heavy sigh*) Do we *have* to talk about this?

Father: Please listen to me.

Daughter: Whatever.

Father: When you're young it seems like you can quit smoking whenever you want, but it can be extremely addictive. Before you know it, you're hooked.

Daughter: Can I go now?

Father: I'm not finished.

Daughter: (*Heavy sigh*)

Father: Honey, I care about you. I don't want you to start smoking. Promise me that when a friend of yours offers you a cigarette, you'll politely decline. Just say, "No thank you." Then never talk to that person again for as long as you live. Okay?

Daughter: (*Puts on CD headset*)
Father: Are you listening to me?
Daughter: (*No response*)
Father: (*Carefully reaches out and pulls away one of the earphones, resisting temptation to rip them off and stomp on the CD player*) I'm not through talking to you.
Daughter: (*Shrugs, rolls eyes, sighs, turns up music*)
Father: (*Blood pressure causes steam-whistle sound*)

Pondering my plan of attack on the smoking issue, I thought back to when I was a teenager, when life was much harder and more character building, and realized that my father's tactic of simply telling me that he would kill me if I smoked just wouldn't work here.

No, if I were going to scare my daughter into staying straight, waving my fist in front of her nose wasn't the way to go about it—she knew a feeble bluff when she saw it.

So when my daughter burst in from school the next day, ravenous as always, I was sitting there with a freshly delivered pizza and a masterfully innocuous expression on my face. (Honesty and forthrightness are critical values in the father-daughter relationship and should always be employed unless devious deception will work better.)

She stopped dead when she saw me, frowning suspiciously. "What's going on?" she demanded.

"Nothing." I beamed. "Want some pizza?"

Yes, she wanted it. I could see the feverish hunger in her eyes. Normally when she came home from school she emptied the kitchen cabinets in frantic foraging. She couldn't possibly resist her primary food source when it was right in front of her. Distrust causing her to hesitate only a moment, she snagged a piece and began chewing, watching me carefully.

"Eat up," I encouraged.

"What's going on?" she queried through a full mouth. "Did Mom leave you or something?"

I frowned. "What do you mean by that?"

She shrugged. "It's just that you're acting so . . . friendly."

"Has your mom said anything about leaving me?"

"Forget it."

"Has she talked about anybody?"

"It's okay, you're back to normal now."

I let her gorge herself on pizza. When she pushed the final piece away, I stood up. "Let's go outside," I suggested.

A look of alarm crossed her face. "Why? What's up?"

"Nothing. I just want to talk to you for a minute."

"I'm not raking the leaves."

"No, it's not about that."

"If it's about leaving your bike out in the rain, it wasn't my fault."

"What? You mean you left my . . ." I took a deep breath, resolving to stay on mission. "No, it's not about that. I just want to talk."

"I don't want to talk. Talk about what?"

"Nothing bad."

She stood up, curious but afraid. "I have to do homework."

"Come on, this will just take a minute."

We went out into the backyard. She stopped when she saw the excavations my stupid dog had industriously dug around the bushes. Apparently my canine believes that if its owners spend so much time fussing around the roots of the expensive shrubbery, there must be something edible buried there. "Those holes are not my fault," my daughter warned me.

"I know."

"I shouldn't have to fill them in. That's not my job."

"Let's go sit on the trampoline," I suggested.

A trampoline is a device for catapulting children through the air and onto their craniums. There is absolutely no good reason to own such a thing, and when my kids suggested we buy one, I issued an Absolute Veto against it, so they bought me one for Father's Day.

The black surface of the trampoline was warmed by the sun, almost uncomfortably hot as we bounced ourselves into a sitting position. I reached into a pocket and pulled out the pack of cigarettes.

"Oh," she murmured. A flicker of worry passed through her eyes before they turned cold. "What were you doing in my room?"

"I was looking for a floppy disk. You told me I could get one from your desk," I reminded her.

She ran her hand through her hair. "That was . . . last *week*." She slid her legs over to the side of the trampoline, preparing to dismount. "You can't go through my things. It's my *room*."

"Where did you get these?" I asked in a conversational tone.

"They belong to a *friend*," she hissed.

"A friend." I let that one bounce around on the trampoline for a while, then brought out a lighter. "Okay."

My daughter's eyes bulged. "What are you doing?" she demanded.

"I thought we could try smoking together."

"What?"

"I think your friend gave these to you for a reason. You want to try smoking, let's try smoking. You and me."

"Are you *serious*?"

"Very." I fumbled with the paper tube, eventually managing to ignite it and a small amount of eyebrow. "Here." I passed it to her and lit another.

We sat there tensely, staring at each other. Her cigarette bobbed nervously in her hand, the smoke tracing out an erratic EKG in the air. "Take a puff," I urged.

"Why are we doing this?" she whispered, her suspicion set to maximum.

"Rather than put you in a position of possibly disobeying your father, which I know you would never willingly do, ever, under any circumstances, I thought it would make sense if you smoked with special secret permission."

Her look indicated that she might have already been in a position of disobeying her father once or twice in her life, but if she had, she was going to keep it a special secret.

"Go ahead, suck it in," I suggested. Her cheeks hollowed as she drew in the unfamiliar pollution. Her face adopted the expression of someone who has accidentally swallowed a mouse, and she began projectile coughing.

"Pretty good, huh?"

I could see her teenage mind calculating as she regarded the smoldering tip of the poison delivery system in her hand.

She hadn't realized that her lungs would react so vehemently to the insertion of carbonized tobacco into their sensitive walls, and knew that if she were ever going to be cool in front of her friends, she was going to have to master her biological responses. With a frown of determination, she took another drag, leaning forward a second later and barking the smoke out of her mouth, nose, and eyes.

"It's better if you breathe it in deep," I advised solemnly.

She glanced at me trustingly, and it nearly broke my heart.

Halfway through the second cigarette, her body seemed to resign itself to the abuse. Her cheeks flushed as the nicotine or the oxygen deprivation stimulated the capillaries that were surviving the assault. "Have another," I offered generously.

She was getting into it now. Instead of gripping the cigarette like a pencil, she was waving it insouciantly through the air between two sophisticated fingers. She was able to ignite the next one in line from the coals of the first, shooting me a triumphant little smile.

My own cigarette was burning itself out without aid from my lungs—when I held the thing to my lips, I did so without inhaling, like Clinton trying marijuana. "Says on the side of the packet here that prolonged use of this product can lead to huge jury awards," I remarked.

Her laugh sounded like two dry sticks being rubbed together. "Maybe next week we'll do heroin," I suggested. I stood up. "Want to jump on the trampoline a little?"

My movement toppled her over. She held the cigarette away from her body as she righted herself back into a cross-legged position. "Not really," she told me.

"Well . . . ," I said. I flexed my knees a little, sending tremors across the taut surface of the tramp. She put a trembling hand out to steady herself. Sensing I was ready to give up on our little adventure, she sucked furiously at the cigarette, like someone making a last run at the dinner buffet before it closed.

I launched myself higher.

Something seemed to be changing the nature of the experience for her. It was as if her body, unable to convince her to stop this nonsense by merely serving up lung spasms, had now decided to throw some other internal organs into the fray. "Hey, could you quit bouncing for a minute?" she said.

"Just one more," I promised her.

The heat coming off the trampoline was palpable, though I suspected the sudden sheen of sweat on her forehead was due more to interior mechanisms. She began crawling to the side of the trampoline, her face an interesting shade of gray-green. When she dropped to the ground, her legs trembled as if she'd landed in the middle of an earthquake, and I could sense that her brain still thought it was on the trampoline.

I slid down to terra firma and put my arm around her. "You okay?"

She nodded bravely but clung to me as I half led, half carried her to bed. She hit the covers like a sack of laundry being thrown from a truck, her hands gripping the sheets in an effort to keep the room from spinning.

Listening to her raspy breathing, I was pretty sure that when she roused herself from her coma, she would face the world as a nonsmoker.

The Trial of my Older Daughter

The Honorable W. Bruce Cameron Presiding

Judge Father: Please be seated. In the matter of the state versus my older daughter, for the crimes of burglary, theft, and destruction of property, are we ready to proceed?

Younger Daughter: Prosecution is ready, Your Honor.

Judge Father: Very well. And the defendant has chosen to represent herself in this matter?

Older Daughter: Yes, Your Honor.

Judge Father: Let's proceed with opening statements.

Younger Daughter: Thank you. The state will prove beyond a reasonable doubt that the defendant did knowingly and willingly enter my bedroom and go into my closet and remove a pair of blue jeans that I paid for with my own money, and take said jeans back to her bedroom, where she maliciously destroyed them. If we allow this sort of crime to go unpunished, next she'll be taking Dad's sweatshirt and wearing it when he is out of town, which she did two weeks ago.

Older Daughter: Hey!

Judge Father: You have an objection?

Older Daughter: We're not supposed to be talking about anything but the blue jeans.

Judge Father: I'm going to allow a little leeway in the opening statement, particularly since I told you to stop wearing my sweatshirts.

Older Daughter: I move that the judge disqualify himself on the grounds that he is prejudiced against me.

Judge Father: I am not prejudiced against you, I am prejudiced against having my clothing disappear. Let's move along. Do you have an opening statement?

Older Daughter: Yes.

Judge Father: Well?

Older Daughter: What's the use? You won't listen anyway.

Judge Father: I'm listening. Do you want to proceed, or not?

Older Daughter: Okay. Well, first, she's a big baby, and how can it be burglary if the stereo is turned up in her room, which *Dad says* you can't do, so if you have to go in there to turn it off, which I do all the time and nobody thanks me for that, and if you want to talk about sweatshirts, what about when Adam came over and you let him ride Dad's bicycle and I never said anything *malicious* about that, and maybe if you paid me back the money you owed me, which I asked for and you were such a snot, none of this would have happened.

Judge Father: Interesting opening statement. Will you be pleading insanity?

Older Daughter: This is just so unfair.

Judge Father: Okay. First witness?

Younger Daughter: The prosecution calls its only witness, my brother.

Judge Father: Son, do you swear to tell the truth, the whole truth, and nothing but the truth?

Son: Okay.

Judge Father: You may be seated.

Son: I've seen them both wearing your sweatshirts, Dad.

Younger Daughter: Objection!

Older Daughter: Oh-oh, now who's going to jail?

Son: Well, he said to tell the whole truth.

Judge Father: That's fine, but let's stick to one case at a time.

Son: Okay.

Younger Daughter: Now, please tell the court in your own words what happened last Sunday afternoon, when you saw the defendant enter my bedroom, go into the closet, take out a pair of brand-new blue jeans, and go into her own bedroom?

Judge Father: Those don't sound like his own words.

Older Daughter: Yeah, objection to that!

Judge Father: Sustained. Please refrain from leading the witness.

Younger Daughter: Yes, Your Honor. What happened Sunday afternoon?

Son: I was sitting on the floor watching television.

Judge Father: Wait a minute. A perfectly good Sunday afternoon and all you can think of to do is watch TV?

Son: Well, how else was I supposed to witness the crime?

Older Daughter: I'm telling you, there was no crime.

Judge Father: Just go on with your story, though let it be noted for the record that the court may find a list of chores to do next Sunday that will serve as a good substitute for television.

Son: Oh great, I knew this would happen.

Judge Father: Please continue with your testimony.

Son: Well, I'm sitting there because *I had just finished doing my chores and Mom said I could watch television,* and she goes in and takes the blue jeans.

Younger Daughter: Let the record show that the witness is indicating the defendant.

Judge Father: So ordered.

Younger Daughter: If it please the court, the people would like to enter into evidence this pair of blue jeans.

Older Daughter: What people?

Judge Father: Admitted into evidence as people's exhibit A.

Younger Daughter: Now, let me ask you, are these the jeans that she stole from me?

Son: Yep.

Younger Daughter: And she cut them off to make shorts?

Son: Yep.

Younger Daughter: And now they're ruined. These were my best blue jeans!

Older Daughter: What a baby.

Judge Father: Let me see those. Well, my God, did you really think you were going to be able to wear these like this? They're so short they're . . . they're . . . gynecological! Are you out of your mind?

Older Daughter: Well, what's the use of this if you think I'm guilty without even hearing my side of the story?

Judge Father: I . . . okay, I'm speaking of these cutoffs here, and merely noting that any daughter of mine who attempts to wear something like this will be grounded.

Older Daughter: I never said I wore them, did I? This is like one of those courts for Captain Kangaroo.

Judge Father: The defendant is warned to refrain from sarcastic remarks or she will be held in contempt of court. Does the prosecution have anything further?

Younger Daughter: No further questions, Your Honor.

Judge Father: Very well, your witness.

Older Daughter: Okay. So you say you were watching television.

Son: Uh-huh, because my chores were already done.

Older Daughter: Yet you saw me go into her room.

Son: Uh-huh.

Older Daughter: So tell me, how did you see me when you were facing the television?

Son: I turned around.

Older Daughter: No you didn't! You just sat there!

Son: Well, but I heard you breathing.

Older Daughter: What?

Son: I could tell it was you because of your breathing.

Older Daughter: That's completely stupid.

Son: Hey, can she call me stupid?

Judge Father: Does the state object?

Younger Daughter: Well, it is kind of stupid.

Judge Father: Son, you're saying you didn't see anything, right?

Son: Right.

Judge Father: Well then, there are no witnesses to the alleged crime.

Younger Daughter: What? You think I did this to my *own* jeans?

Judge Father: No, but I can't find for the prosecution based on breathing.

Older Daughter: Ha!

Younger Daughter: What about the fact that I found the jeans lying on her bed?

Older Daughter: So who's the burglar now?

Judge Father: Were they on your bed?

Older Daughter: Well yeah, but that doesn't mean I put them there. Nobody heard me *breathing*.

Judge Father: All right, I'm ready to render a verdict.

Older Daughter: Just a second! Does anybody care that she owes me twenty dollars that if she had paid me I was going to buy a pair of shorts that were on sale?

Younger Daughter: That doesn't give you the right to just steal my jeans!

Judge Father: All right, I'm ready to make a decision here.

Older Daughter: Well, okay, but I had to have a pair of shorts! I was going to the park to play Frisbee with Blaine.

Younger Daughter: Blaine Petersen? Ohmygod, he is so hot. Are you going out with him?

Judge Father: The court will now pronounce judgment.

Older Daughter: No, he's going out with Cecilia, but you *know* she's going to get back with Jake. She talks about him like all the time.

Younger Daughter: She is such a bitch.

Judge Father: Hey! What did you just say?

Older Daughter: I'm sorry about your jeans, but I was desperate.

Younger Daughter: I'll pay you back the money I owe you, but you have to buy me a new pair of jeans.

Judge Father: Does no one care about the verdict?

Older Daughter: That's fair.

Younger Daughter: Want to go to the mall? We could find some shorts.

Older Daughter: And I think they're having a sale on jeans at the Gap.

Younger Daughter: Okay.

Son: Dad, can I play judge now?

Conclusion

Psychologists often advocate taking a carrot-and-stick approach to raising teenagers, though I can't imagine what good it could possibly do to hit someone with a carrot. For parents, the purpose of punishment is to convince themselves that despite evidence to the contrary, they are doing a good job of raising their children. For teenagers, punishment is only an unpleasant reminder that they were caught—it isn't really going to impact their behavior one way or another.

My daughters have even tried, on occasion, to implement a sort of barter system when it comes to discipline.

Older Daughter: (*Loud party noises in the background*) Dad, is Mom there?

Father: She can't come to the phone.

Older Daughter: Oh.

Father: Is there something I can do for you?

Older Daughter: Well, remember when you told me I couldn't go to the party at Amanda's house just because her parents are out of town, which has like nothing to do with it?

Father: I remember.

Older Daughter: Well, what would the punishment be if I came here anyway?

Father: You'd be grounded for a week. No phone, no car, and your room would have to be clean before you could go out again.

Older Daughter: (*Long pause*) How about if I'm just grounded from the car and I'll clean my room?

It's frustrating to think that throughout history, man has trained horses and dogs and even lions but no one has ever successfully trained a teenager. Teenage girls believe their behavior is justified because if they didn't rebel against you, they wouldn't be teenagers. Punishment seems ineffective, but what else are you going to do? You can't just give up. That would upset the natural order. You're both stuck in your roles. They're the teenage daughters, and you: you're the father.

Unauthorized Physical Changes

At a Certain Age, a Teenage Girl Begins Displaying Disturbing Reminders as to Why We Are Called Mammals

Few things are more distressing to a father than to watch as the lovely features of his little girl become all distorted by the rampaging hormonal conspiracies of the teenage body. Fortunately, there is an effective technique a father can use to counter these changes: denial. (You are already denying her permission to act like a grown-up; denying that she looks like one is, in some ways, even easier.)

No one thinks to warn the father that the daughter is about to undergo her radical transformation. It would be helpful if, the moment the bloodstream begins to flood with teenage hormones, an alarm of some kind went off, sort of like what happens when someone scores a goal in hockey.

When it came to my older daughter, the first news I had of impending doom occurred when I innocently suggested on Saturday afternoon that the two of us take the football and practice her pass patterns, which needed some work on their timing. At this point she was in the sixth grade, still eligible for recess, and was one of the few female participants in the daily football game out on the grass. Something about the physical collisions of the sport appealed to her—I could just imagine her lowering her head and running right over the top of some hapless boy standing in her way.

But she didn't want to play. Catching a football had dropped overnight from her list of priorities.

Naturally, I was understanding and patient, though I had to ask her several times what did she *mean* she didn't want to play football anymore, how could you not want to play football, you love football, when she finally blurted:

"I don't like it when they tackle me."

This struck me as completely out of character. Being tackled allowed her to crash her weight down on some unlucky opponent—watching her play in the neighborhood a few times over the years, I got the impression that being tackled was more fun for her than scoring a touchdown.

She explained: "The boys have started to get all grabby."

When I finally understood what she was saying, I felt as if *I* had been tackled. My face went numb, the blood drained from my extremities, I sat down to keep from passing out.

My daughter now had parts that the boys wanted to grab.

Careful not to overreact, I told my daughter we'd toss the ball around some other day, then went inside to look in the phone book for all-girls' schools.

"What are we going to *do*?" I beseeched my wife.

She regarded me with an expression that I've come to learn means she thinks I'm being an idiot. "There's nothing we can do," she advised.

"What do you mean?" I raged calmly. "Of course we can do something! We're her *parents*. I can't believe you're proposing to just stand by and let this happen."

"Well, what do you want to do, post a sign in her room?"

My younger daughter has had less time to develop, but is attempting to hurry the process along with her choice of clothing. The technical term for this is "inappropriate accentuation," and I do my best to bring it to my daughter's attention so that she can rectify her mistake, as in the following exchange.

Reasonable Father: Hey! Where do you think you're going?

Younger Daughter: (*Shrug*) Out.

Reasonable Father: I can see that. But where?

Younger Daughter: (*Sigh*) Katie's coming to pick me up.

Reasonable Father: Okay, can you see that you've answered the wrong question? We'll get into my valid objections as to the "how" in a minute—for now, I'm still interested in the "where."

Younger Daughter: I hate it when you act like this.

Reasonable Father: I notice that in your haste to make your getaway, you accidentally put on too small a T-shirt.

Younger Daughter: Can I just go?

Reasonable Father: Not dressed in shrink-wrap, you can't.

Younger Daughter: I hate you! (*Runs to bedroom, slams door, lights an Aspen Meadow candle*)

Reasonable Father: While you're in there, find something looser to wear!

What's Changing

Though I usually do my best not to dwell on the physical changes my teenage daughters have exhibited over the years (Remember: Denial. Learn it. Use it), I will recount them here.

Size

Though it seems like just a few weeks ago your little girl was climbing in your lap to be read a story, you'll notice that her legs have now grown far longer than was previously necessary to reach the ground. She no longer peers up at you as if you were a skyscraper—you're more like the neighborhood bank building, barely taller than she is, and with a certain set of well-defined functions. She looks like she easily weighs over a hundred pounds—you don't even *want* something like that in your lap.

I first recognized my older daughter's new height when I went to the gym to set some volleyballs for her. I tapped the tight white sphere into the air and my daughter leaped up *over* the net and smacked the thing right back at my face. Totally unprepared, I watched stupefied as the streaking missile came at my nose, ending the pain-free portion of the afternoon.

"Are you all right?" my daughter asked anxiously.

"Of course," I assured her lightly. "No problem."

"Then why are you lying down?"

"Sleepy."

"Are you going to get back up?"

"I don't see why not."

"When?"

"As soon as the feeling returns to my legs."

Having larger children can be useful: they can now carry in groceries and help with yard work. Not that they will actually do these things, you understand—it's just that they *can*.

Acne

The day the first pimple enters the household on the face of a teenage daughter there is much hysterical raving. Your daughter locks herself in her bedroom, sobbing, while the rest of the family gathers on the other side of the door in concern.

"I'm never coming out. Never!" she wails.

"While you're in there, why don't you pick up a little?" you suggest helpfully. Everyone in the family gives you a look of sheer disgust.

"She can't. She has acne," you're told.

Sirens blazing, the family races off to the pharmacy to purchase an array of antiacne treatments—enough chemicals to destroy the ozone layer in a single application.

"Try this. The label is in French and it was extremely expensive," your wife babbles. "It's the secretion of a pregnant albino platypus."

"All this stuff goes on *top* of the skin. Acne comes from *below* the skin," you argue. "Would you use a *gel* to treat appendicitis?"

Inserting logic into this particular hostage crisis is not

appreciated—your daughter wants sympathy, not dermatology.

Your wife grabs the *Home Emergency Medical Reference Guide* and starts calling things through the door. "Try applying hot compresses!" she suggests.

"Do you mean to tell me that acne is considered an emergency medical condition?" you demand. Has the entire world gone crazy?

"It says here that if you get a bit of sunburn, it can get rid of pimples!" your wife says.

There's a pause in the hysterical sobbing. "Really?"

"I guess, though, that if you're not leaving your room, that leaves *that* out," you observe. Everyone is staring at you again. "What?"

"You're not helping," your wife informs you.

"What do you mean? I'm here, part of the Pimple Emergency Response Team, aren't I? You're in charge of overreaction, I'm in charge of sanity."

"You're the one who always overreacts, Dad," your younger daughter advises archly.

"You do seem to have problems adjusting to the fact that your daughter is becoming a woman," your wife agrees psychiatrically.

"That's the most ridiculous thing I've ever heard in my life. She is *not* becoming a woman!"

"Are you still there?" your older daughter sniffs.

"Don't worry, we're still panicking," you reply. "We're just doing it more quietly."

"Do you want to try getting a little sun, dear?" your wife wants to know. "Maybe that will help."

"Or a tanning booth?" comes the voice on the other side of the door.

"That's right. We have a perfectly good sun up there in the sky for free, so let's run off and pay forty bucks a visit to a tanning salon," you reason.

"You can save twenty dollars if you buy three in advance," your younger daughter advises.

"Oh, well, if you can save *twenty* dollars . . ."

"If I'm going to go to a tanning salon, I'm going to need a new bathing suit," your older daughter warns.

You will feel your patience being sapped by all this negotiating. Maybe later you should take a video of your daughter's bedroom door so that years from now you can better remember what it was like to talk to her as a teenager. "I thought sun causes wrinkles anyway," you shout.

"Yeah, when you're, like, thirty years *old*," your younger daughter sneers. "By then, who cares what you look like, your life is over anyway."

Well, that's a good point.

PMS—Precarious Mental Situation

Apparently the two weeks before and the two weeks after a woman has what my mother used to call "the curse" are a difficult time, resulting in satanic mood swings. I really don't want to dwell on what causes this syndrome, whose effects are suffered equally by the teenage daughter and the rest of the family. I only know that out of the blue, you will find yourself having conversations like this.

> **Father:** Did you run all the water out of the hot water heater again? It's hotter than Ethiopia in the bathroom! Other people need to take a shower, you know!
>
> **Daughter:** I hate you! (*Bursts into tears, locks herself in bathroom, runs shower*)

One of the more frustrating aspects of PMS is that men are not allowed to mention its existence. When the daughter jumps up from the dinner table, shrieking that it is not anyone's business that she has homework, the wife will look at her perplexed husband and say, "It's just her period."

"I don't want to know," the father will reply honestly.

When the exact same thing happens a month later, the father turns to his wife and asks, "Is it her period?"

"What an insensitive thing to say!" the wife will snap. "Just like a man!"

Eventually it will occur to you that there is a biological function under way here whose purpose is not merely to drive you crazy but also to prepare your daughter for reproduction. This realization will usually take place in the dead of night, causing you to sit bolt upright, as if you've just heard someone breaking into your house.

Be careful not to overreact. If you go charging into your daughter's bedroom to make sure she is alone in there, you are likely to trip over a mound of clothes on her floor and possibly break an ankle. Just because it has only just occurred to you that your daughter now has the physical ability to get pregnant doesn't mean it's actually happening at that moment. Try to get some sleep—there will be plenty of time in the morning to think about barbed wire, German shepherds, and other reasonable protections.

Hair

There is an evolutionary purpose to hair: it covers the head. Without it, people tend to suffer from chill, sunburns, and an obsessive belief that "women find bald men very sexy." (This last seems to be the conclusion of a polling sample that excluded any actual women.) Teenagers don't seem to be aware that your hair is there for a reason; in fact, they seem to want to torment their hair. They twirl it, tease it, color it, stress it with hot clamps and steaming tubes, and even put it in their mouths. Fathers maintain a helpful running commentary on these behaviors, instructing their daughters in a fashion that is both compelling and ignored.

When they are not playing with their hair, teenage daughters are talking about it.

> **Heather:** Ohmygod! Did you color your hair?
> **Older Daughter:** Yes! It was Mild October Dawn and now it's Serene Autumn Morning."
> **Heather:** I love it! I'm so jealous, I can only stick to the muted ebonies because I'm a winter.

(This is what she said—I don't pretend to understand it.)

My younger daughter doesn't waste words gushing about her hair, though she experiments with it more, going with what I suppose Heather would call one of the stark ebonies along with a shock in her bangs of what appears to be Strident Chernobyl.

"Do you hate your head or something?" I demand. She refuses to answer on the grounds that I'm being accurate.

In order to manage her hair, the teenage girl needs more equipment than a TV repairman. Spoked implements live all over the bathroom counter, hissing vapor whenever the father attempts to move them aside.

My wife is no help when it comes to hair—as long as it's clean, she says it's cute.

"Remember when they had pigtails? Now *that* was cute," I tell her.

Body Hair

The first indication a father will have that his daughter is starting to sprout body hair is when he goes to shave in the morning and his face is left in tatters by a razor blade that has been thoroughly warped and distorted by several trips up and down his daughter's legs. Looking like he's stuck his head in front of a sandblaster, he'll confront his daughter, who will act as if it is his fault because he didn't think to buy her a personal razor.

It won't take long before a girl decides that no sliver of steel is adequate to the task of removing all vestiges of hair, and she'll bring home some bikini wax. Prepare yourself; you've never heard such screaming. Bikini wax functions by lifting an entire layer of live skin from the body in a single ripping motion. The first time your daughter tries it, you'll assume someone is the victim of a chain-saw massacre, and you'll run to the bathroom door and pound on it. "What's going on?" you'll demand.

"I'm waxing!" she'll sob.

"What?" Fathers should put the appropriate amount of perplexity in their voices. "If you want to wax something, why don't you work on my car?"

This will earn you more hard looks from everyone in the family, though all you were trying to do was spare your daughter pain.

Even Worse Changes

Perhaps the most distressing change in a daughter's body during the teenage years occurs in the chest area, where without warning a girl will begin to sprout protuberances.

There are few things more distressing to a father than when his daughter begins protuberating. To be honest, we'd really rather deploy our paternal denial mechanism than face the truth about what's going on, but most of us have spent a lifetime training our eyes to gravitate toward similar objects when they are thrust at us by other women, and it proves nearly impossible to ignore them on our own daughters. Even worse, boys will come over and practically burn a hole in your daughters' shirts, unable to do anything but stare in openmouthed wonder. A father's protective instincts will compel him to take action when this happens, doing everything from stepping in as a physical barrier between his daughters and these slobbering boys to racing over to call the Our Lady of Sin Nunnery in Richmond, Indiana, to see if they accept emergency admissions.

The important thing is not to panic, because if you do, you'll never *not* be panicking again—now that they are here, your daughters' chest developments are not going away.

Brace Yourself for Braces

A little girl's teeth are straight and even. You'd think that when the adult teeth come in, they would simply fill the slots left over by these perfect little baby teeth, but that would be easy and inexpensive, two words that are incompatible with having a teenage daughter. The same hormones that are wracking the body with severe changes send signals to the teeth and order them to rebel, so that as they come in they are as disorganized and angry as a teenager's bedroom.

The solution is obvious: braces, the most expensive metal on earth, must be inserted into the mouth to squelch the rebellion.

Our orthodontist is a well-fed-looking fellow who herds us all into a back room so no one can overhear my reaction to his estimate. "Now then, Mr. Cameron, are you comfortable?"

"No."

"Are you ready to discuss your daughter's treatment?"

"No."

"Very well. Your daughter has a severe overbite." He regards her jaw lovingly. "She has an expensive separation of teeth in the front, and pricey misalignment of the bicuspid. There are also some costly areas where her teeth are coming in a bit skewed, in what we call the 'extra dental income syndrome.' We'll do asset depletion on the lower teeth first, followed by bank account draining on the uppers a month later. I assume you'll be getting a second job?"

I grunt with the pain of my impending walletectomy.

"Here, let me show you some pictures." He snaps on a light and unfurls a large photograph. "Here's the sailboat I'll be buying as a result of your daughter's orthodontia."

"Do you have those braces that look like diamonds?" my daughter wants to know.

He chuckles. "Of course, dear. We can even use real diamonds, if you'd like."

"That would be nice," everyone agrees.

"Can we install a feature that allows me to wire her mouth shut when I want?" I ask.

He gives me a sour look. "Mr. Cameron, we do not joke when it comes to our children's teeth. I have problems enough with my tax bracket without you coming in here acting like a wise guy."

"Sorry."

The first step in the process is to take an impression of my mouth so that I can be fitted with a rubber guard that will prevent me from damaging my teeth from gritting them when I am handed his estimate. I stare at the number—apparently he is planning to recoup the cost of dental school on a single patient.

"You don't really want braces, do you, dear?" I gasp hoarsely to my daughter.

"Daddy," she replies.

When the metal bands are fixed in place and criss-crossed with rubber bands, I feel a little better. It is hard to picture a teenage boy willingly trying to kiss what looks like a device for shredding lips. Maybe with all this metal inserted between her and her sex appeal, I will have a few years of relative calm.

The first meal after the braces are put in place is rather dramatic, my daughter sobbing and moaning as if trying to win the Academy Award for melodrama. "I can only eat Jell-O!" she wails. When we dutifully prepare Jell-O and set it before her, she pretends it hurts to chew *that*.

"I'm *not* going to school with these things in my mouth," she vows, standing in the bathroom staring at her mouth.

"You look like the Terminator," my son suggests helpfully.

"My life is *over*!" she sobs.

"When the braces come off, you'll have the prettiest smile in the school!" your wife promises, apparently forgetting that our children belong to the Instant Gratification Generation. When they come *off*? Teenagers don't think more than forty-eight hours in the future unless there's a big party coming.

"Maybe by that time, I'll have gotten a big raise, so we can afford food!" I state hopefully.

An hour later, a pack of my daughter's friends arrive to inspect the orthodontia. Because I have trouble telling them apart, I call them all Heather. They swarm around my daughter, asking her questions. "Does it hurt to chew? Does it hurt to swallow? Does it hurt to smile?"

Yes, my daughter tells them, it all hurts.

They admire the way the blue gemstones look, especially in contrast with the green rubber bands. By the time they leave, my daughter is no longer attempting to talk while keeping her lips over her teeth, and she departs for school the next morning without incident. For once, I am grateful for the presence of the Heathers.

Conclusion

More swiftly than you can possibly prepare yourself for, the little girl you've been raising is vanishing, the same way her baseball mitt and hockey helmet are disappearing into her closet, never to emerge again. This is plainly a dreadful development, but you'll find little political support in your family when you suggest remedies, such as judiciously applying duct tape to some of the afflicted areas to smooth out some of the bumps. "It will make for a more aerodynamic appearance," you'll argue to no avail. Teenage girls don't want to be aerodynamic, they want to stop traffic.

All you can do in this situation is stand on the other side of the locked door and shout reasonable advice, which will be ignored, or establish a set of reasonable new rules to deal with recent developments, which will be ignored. You don't get a vote in any of this. It's a plot by three women—your daughter, your wife, and Mother Nature—to radically alter the rules by which you've been playing all along (the most important rule being, nothing happens without Dad's permission). It's almost as if you're irrelevant to this whole process, which is patently ridiculous. How can your opinion about your own daughter's physical changes not matter? You're the father!

Feeding Your Teenage Daughter

The Family Dinner—Just Because Other People Do This Doesn't Mean You Should Too

After surviving on little more than animal-shaped break-fast cereal for twelve years, the metabolism of a teen-ager stirs and then wakens with a roar, sending the family food budget fleeing for its life. As often as her bedroom door is slammed, the cupboard door is open, the teenager staring ravenously at the contents.

"What are you doing? We eat dinner in an hour," you say.

"I'm hungry *now*," she states vehemently, pulling out a box of instant pudding and scowling at the instructions. "Hey, this isn't *instant*, you have to like boil water."

"You can wait for dinner," you respond firmly.

"No I *can't*." The look she gives you sends chills up your spine: you are suddenly reminded that in some species, it is quite common for the old and sick to be eaten by their young. (Okay, I can't actually think of an animal that does this, but it's still a creepy thought.)

My daughters have mastered the skill of eating that second hamburger I had my eye on and complaining that "we never have anything good for dinner" at the same time.

Fathers who point out the irony in this situation will receive a scornful look in response. Teenagers don't do irony.

Unless you serve nothing but chocolate for dinner, teenagers will utter bitter denouncements at every meal. "I hate Italian food," they mutter. "Everything Italian tastes terrible. I wish we'd never even *discovered* Italy!"

"That's just crazy," you respond instructionally. "If you lived in Italy, you'd grow *up* eating Italian food. Dinner wouldn't be Italian food, it would just be 'food.' Would you sit around saying, 'I hate food? All food tastes terrible'?"

This beautifully composed logic is ignored.

"What's for dessert?" your teenagers demand in response. "Do we have any pudding?"

Fathers who point out that the meal was procured by money that the parents earned, and that if the children are going to continue to make gag-reflex expressions at every mouthful, maybe they ought to consider getting a job and paying for some groceries themselves, will receive a scornful look in return. Teenagers don't do economics.

Planning the Menu for the Week

I am a modern American male, fully involved in the cooking of meals in my house even when my children lovingly demand I stop because they "can't stand all the smoke." From the moment that the odors begin emerging from the kitchen, where my wife's handiwork is bubbling on the stove or baking in the oven, I am on hand to assist. Often I'll pick up a ladle and sample some sauce, offering constructive criticism—my wife, perhaps a bit jealous of my talent in this area, accepts these kind words with poor grace. I'll direct the children in setting the table, and after the meal, as I'm settled comfortably in my chair, I'll take time away from the television to supervise the kitchen cleanup.

Few activities are as pleasant for me as the creation of the menus for the week. The excitement of all those dinners to come makes me positively joyous. This is one area where I am perfectly content to handle the entire task myself, laboring over a balanced plan and handing it to my wife, who often tells me I should consider cooking the meals myself. I accept her jest with good humor.

Unfortunately, the older children become, the more they feel they should have a voice in what the family eats, and they begin attempting to insinuate themselves in the meal planning process. It makes a father long for the days when a child could be strapped into a tall chair and force-fed stewed carrots, little eyes watching the tiny spoon circling around in the air while Daddy made rocket noises. I can recall fondly the look of amazement on their faces that something that looked as bad as stewed carrots could taste as bad as stewed carrots.

When my wife fed the babies, she always spooned some of the wretched paste into her own mouth, which I considered to be just sick.

So now it is Sunday, and I am at the table, a pad of paper spread cleanly out in front of me, waiting for me to write down the dinners I would like for each of the coming days. Just as I lift my pen, I am ambushed.

"What are you doing, Dad?" my son wants to know.

I glare at him suspiciously. He never wants to know what I am doing. "Planning chores," I reply shortly. "I'm glad you're here, we need to put down a new layer of asphalt on the driveway."

"Is it the meals for the week?" he asks, coming around to read the heading "Meals for the Week" written across the top of the page.

"No."

As if by sheer coincidence, my two daughters appear at my elbow. "We think *we* should plan the meals this week," my oldest child explains. They sit down as if we're getting ready to play a card game.

"Well, you're wrong," I advise them kindly.

"Mom says she's not going to cook anything unless we all agree on it. She says she's sick of everybody complaining."

What? "Who complains? I don't know what you're talking about," I sputter.

"You always pick bad food, Dad," my son tells me.

I take a deep breath. "Okay, fine. Let's do it together, then. Monday, I was thinking lasagna."

"Gross!" they howl, clutching their stomachs and dropping to the floor as if felled by kidney stones. I watch them writhing around, my eyes cold and unamused.

"If we have to have Italian, I vote for SpaghettiOs," my son declares.

"SpaghettiOs! That's not Italian. That's not even *food*," I object.

"Well, macaroni and cheese, then."

"I say pizza," my older daughter asserts.

"Pizza," my younger daughter echoes.

"Pizza," my son agrees.

Reluctantly, I write it down, and the children share triumphant grins. "Tuesday," I state cautiously.

"I'm a vegetarian," my younger daughter informs me suddenly and, in my opinion, irrelevantly.

"Since when?" her sister wants to know, wrinkling her nose scornfully. For her, the lack of challenge involved in picking fruit from trees is reason alone to remain carnivorous. If we didn't live in the suburbs, she would probably spend her days hunting and killing her own bison. "You eat meat all the time."

"That's not true. I don't believe animals should be sacrificed for our convenience," my younger daughter huffs.

"Oh, like they do a big *sacrifice*," my older daughter scoffs.

"You disgust me."

"If you are so against killing animals, what are you *wearing*?" my older daughter hoots triumphantly.

My younger daughter fingers her shirt, frowning. "Cotton?"

There's a silence while my older daughter ponders this information.

"SpaghettiOs is vegetarian," my son offers hopefully. "Can we have that on Tuesday?"

"I don't want Italian two days in a row," my older daughter objects.

"SpaghettiOs is not Italian!" I shout. "I don't even think pizza is Italian!"

"Oh, like what, it's Russian?" my younger daughter sneers.

"How about lobster?" my son compromises.

"Yeah, lobster!" my older daughter gushes.

"I'd eat lobster," my younger daughter says.

"Lobster is, after all, one of the healthier vegetables," I observe.

"Tuesday. Lobster," my older daughter writes.

"Wait a minute! We can't afford lobster. Do you know how much lobster *costs*?"

"We'll save money by not buying any beer this week," my older daughter counters.

"Now you're talking crazy," I tell her. "No lobster. That's final."

With a heavy sigh and a roll of her eyes, she marks out Tuesday's entry.

"How about beef Stroganoff?" I suggest.

The children react as if punched in the stomach. "Get off the floor," I bark.

"Dad, no way," my son tells me.

"That's as bad as lasagna," my younger daughter informs me.

"Or remember when we had that pot of boiling stuff and we put the meat in on sticks?"

"Fondue?" I ask.

"Yes!" They fall back on the floor.

"Or chicken pot pie!" my son hoots from his prone position.

"Scalloped potatoes!"

"Stew!"

"Look, I hate to interrupt a rousing game of Meals We Hate, but can we get back to planning the week? We're only on Tuesday and all this talk is making me hungry."

They settle back in their chairs. "I vote we do McDonald's on Tuesday," my son blurts.

"Great idea!" my older daughter agrees.

"That's not vegetarian," I warn.

My younger daughter frowns. "Well, I'm okay with it," she decides.

"What?"

"Tuesday. McDonald's," my older daughter says, writing it down.

"No way," I tell them.

"It's cheaper than lobster, Dad," my son informs me helpfully.

"Either lobster or McDonald's," my older daughter agrees.

I sigh. "Okay, but that's it for fast food," I tell them.

"Okay," my son says.

"Okay," my older daughter says.

"Now. Wednesday," I begin, wondering how to get us back on the subject of chicken pot pie.

"Pizza," my younger daughter interrupts.

"Pizza," her sister agrees.

"Pizza," my son nods.

They write it down.

"I said no more fast food!" I object.

"You think pizza is fast?" my older daughter challenges. "It takes like half an hour."

"But we're having it on Monday!" I shout.

"Thursday." My older daughter ignores me. "What do we want to do Thursday?"

"Hot dogs," my son declares.

"No way," my younger daughter sniffs. "Do you know what goes *in* hot dogs?"

"Actually, I *like* hot dogs," I offer.

That seems to settle it. "Okay, not hot dogs. What else?" my older daughter asks.

"Chinese takeout?" my son wants to know.

"Vegetarian egg rolls," my younger daughter agrees. "Tofu."

"*Tofu?*" I sputter.

"We'll have Chinese on Thursday," my older daughter states, writing it down.

"Did you people know we have a kitchen in this house?" I ask them.

"Friday is pizza night," my older daughter states.

"Pizza."

"Pizza."

I bury my head in my hands.

"Saturday obviously I'll have a date," my older daughter declares. "So you are on your own."

"I'm spending the night at Greta's," my younger daughter agrees.

"I'll be at Jon's house," my son chimes in.

They look at me expectantly. "Lasagna," I state forcefully. They nod placatingly. "Whatever, Dad. Just don't leave any leftovers," my older daughter warns me.

"As if he ever does *that*," my younger daughter sneers.

"What does that mean?" I demand. "Quit laughing."

"That just leaves Sunday," my older daughter says.

"How about pizza?" my son suggests brightly, as if no one has ever uttered the word before in this house.

The children think this is a good idea, and write it down.

The Family Dinner

From the very first time that a child joins the table, the entire nature of the evening meal changes. Gone forever are the romantic, candlelit dinners that you and your wife always meant to have. The sole focus becomes the little dictator in the high chair, who decides for the whole family how the evening will progress. You stop having conversations and instead just make observations. "Oh-oh, he's going for the mashed potatoes." Look at a couple out to eat with a baby in a restaurant—the only way you know they are a family is that they are all wearing the same food.

Teenagers dominate dinnertime in much the same fashion, though it is true that parents are less likely to be sprayed with strained peas.

Ten minutes after the meal has been served, the front door will bang open as if a SWAT team has arrived. The teenager will barge in, demanding to know how come we're having dinner so early and why did we start eating without her, that is really rude.

This is how she apologizes for being late.

After the usual condemnation of whatever was cooked, the teenager will want to know if she can turn on the television to watch her favorite show. In this instance, "favorite" is a floating adjective, used lavishly whenever the teenager feels it strengthens her rhetorical position—as in, "You've ruined my favorite blouse!" wailed from the laundry room, or "Someone ate the last doughnut, those are my favorite!" bellowed from the kitchen.

She turns on the favorite television show, which is apparently about boys and girls her age who cannot keep their lips off each other. They all look the same, which is to say young and flawless, and I have trouble tracking the plot, if there is one. Apparently a boy, I think his name is Spleen, is dating a girl named Fantasia, but Spleen also keeps exchanging scorching glances with the girl's mother, who looks like she is the same age as everyone else on this show. As a subplot, Spleen's brother, Burnt, has a fatal disease that has absolutely no physical symptoms except it causes him to be somewhat mournful.

At commercial, I seize the remote control and exercise my total and complete parental authority by clicking off the show. It recedes into a small white dot in the center of the screen while my children howl their protests. "Why can't we watch TV?" they demand.

"No television unless your homework is done," I declare.

"My homework is done," my older daughter responds.

"Mine too," says my son.

"Mine too," agrees my younger daughter.

"That doesn't matter," I say wisely. The children exchange Dad-is-demented-again looks, but I've momentarily silenced them.

"There's an old movie on that I wouldn't mind seeing," my wife remarks.

We all stare at her in horror. My wife likes to watch movies that were filmed before they invented plot.

"Doris Day is, like, the complete opposite of what I would ever want to be," my older daughter declares.

"So you'd be Doris *Night*?" my son blurts, howling with hilarity at his own wit.

"You are such a hypocrite, Dad," my younger daughter announces forcefully. I blink in surprise.

"Yeah, you're very Hippocratic," my older daughter piles on.

This additional accusation is also somewhat unexpected.

"You know if there was a game on, we'd be watching TV," my younger daughter seethes.

"I thought we were talking about how much we don't like Doris Day?" I reply, bewildered.

"Dad, if we ever get a piñata, can I be the first one at bat?" my son wants to know.

"Does it make you angry when Dad watches sports on television, honey?" my wife asks in a gentle, psychological tone. I scowl, trying to shut down this ridiculous digression from the main topic with facial commands, but my wife isn't paying attention.

"Never mind," my younger daughter says to her plate, speaking so quietly she is barely audible.

"Why don't we talk about it?" my wife suggests kindly.

But my younger daughter merely stares at her food and shakes her head. This is what it's like, having teenagers at the table.

I notice none of the children are eating the chicken tetrazzini, and declare that we will remain seated at the dinner table until everyone has taken a few token bites. My dog recognizes this as a signal to prowl the perimeter of the table. "Hey, no feeding the dog!" I say.

"We're not," the children protest over the sound of the animal's chewing. The amount of tetrazzini on the table begins a rapid decrease, though I never actually catch my children spooning it to our dog. I do watch as my son, at my insistence, raises his fork to his lips and manages to take a bite of what must be less than a molecule of dinner, chewing enthusiastically for a full minute. "Wow, I'm full," he says after an exaggerated swallow.

"Me too!" his sisters proclaim.

Like frightened deer, they suddenly bolt from the table, but I've seen this trick before and I'm ready. "Hold it! The dishes aren't done!"

"I can't do dishes, I have homework," my older daughter protests.

"Me too," says my son.

"Me too," claims my other daughter.

"I want you to do dishes," I instruct my older daughter.

"Why do I have to do it!" she wails. "This isn't fair!"

"You other two clear the table and put away the milk," I order.

"What are you going to do, just sit there?" my younger daughter wants to know.

"I'm supervising. It's part of the Hippocratic oath. Let's get going," I say.

When my older daughter feels she has been unfairly assigned the task of doing the absolute minimum to help the family, she responds by demonstrating her physical incapability of performing her duty without causing much of what they call in the military "collateral damage." Pots are banged together as if she's trying to warn the neighborhood that the British are coming. Plates get dropped, and silverware somehow gets stuck in the garbage disposal. Perfectly good leftovers are thrown away or fed to the dog. "I'm not cleaning the stove," she declares. "I'm not wiping the counter. I'm not cleaning out the sink, that's not my job."

"It's not my job," says my son.

"It's not my job," says my other daughter.

I lovingly advise my oldest child that cleaning the kitchen means the entire kitchen—there are no safe areas. She dials a friend on the phone to express her outrage, and as she walks about the kitchen the cord sweeps items off the counter and onto the floor. "I'm not picking up the stuff on the floor," she announces. "That's not my job."

A Teenager's Diet—a Journey of Torment for the Whole Family

A teenage girl's weight-loss diet consists mainly of hysteria. It begins with the shrieking declaration that she is too fat, with everyone else in the family expected to gather around and offer clucking reassurances that this is not true. At this point, the father of the family can earn himself scathing looks by offering his observation that his daughter is, indeed, looking a little plump. "How could you say that?" your daughter will wail.

"I'm just agreeing with you," you point out defensively.

The daughter slams her bedroom door and sobs. Your wife stares at you coldly and then shakes her head in disgust. "Nice going, Dad," your younger daughter compliments scornfully.

"What? What'd I say?" you protest. But there is no appeal for justice in this court: you've already been summarily found guilty. It's a good thing you don't have a firing squad in the backyard.

"I'm going on a diet," your daughter announces later that day. "What's for dinner?"

"Beef Stroganoff!" you announce exultantly.

She shakes her head. "Too fattening," she avows.

"How about a salad?" my wife offers solicitously.

"With low-fat dressing?" my daughter suggests.

"Of course."

You'll be shocked to learn later that *everybody* is going on a diet in the family. Your wife will set a plate of lettuce in front of you as if she is serving you real food. "Hey, what is this?" you'll protest. "I'm not trying to lose weight. *She's* the one who needs to lose weight, not me."

More tears. Everyone glares at you.

"Maybe you ought to take a look in the mirror," your younger daughter mutters under her breath.

"What did you say?" you demand.

"You did say your pants were fitting a little tight," your wife will agree.

"Because they shrunk!"

"They were new trousers," your wife responds.

"Let's just stay focused on what we're interested in, which is that we can't eat just salad for dinner," you sternly advise her.

"Why do you feel every meal must involve a dead bovine?" your younger daughter challenges.

This is an entirely inappropriate conversation for your family to be having. You sigh, summoning up your patience. "Look. We can't just eat lettuce. We'll starve."

"Oh, I don't think you have to worry about that for a while yet," your younger teenager says.

"When people get older, their metabolisms slow down, and they don't need to eat as much food," your wife tells you kindly. You sort through this statement carefully, searching for relevance. "It wouldn't hurt you to shed a few pounds," she adds.

Suddenly you see through her treachery: she's talking about *you*! Somehow the conversation has shifted from your chubby daughter to your own physique. It's an ambush!

"Maybe you could do some exercise as well," your wife continues, as if you are unaware of the dagger in your back. "And cut back on beer."

Cut back on beer! See how insane conversations like this can become in such a short period of time?

"You need to eat more fruits and vegetables," your younger daughter advises. "All this beef isn't good for you. It's bad for your heart."

This is a girl who tells you she wants to backpack across the country this summer with a boy named Thug (or something like that), and she's *worried about your heart?*

"I don't think you know what you're talking about," you respond. "Look, let's think about this rationally. What do cows eat?"

The dumbfounded expressions on everyone's faces tells you that you've seized the upper hand. You strain to prevent yourself from appearing gleeful.

"Grass?" your son guesses.

"Exactly. And corn! Which are . . . ," you prompt.

Everyone is staring at you.

"Which are . . . ," you state again.

"Crunchy?" your son suggests.

"Animal . . . mineral . . . ," you hint.

"Vegetable," your wife finishes, in a flat tone that suggests she knows where you are going with this.

"Exactly!" you hoot. "So when you eat beef, you are just delivering vegetables to your system in a more efficient format!"

Apparently, no one can deny this. They gape at you in wonder.

"Beer is a beverage made entirely from grains, hops, and, um, foam," you continue, fighting a sob in your throat. This is not the time to get emotional, but this subject always makes you tear up. "These are all natural ingredients, the purest form of nature. As Benjamin Franklin said, beer is proof that God loves us and wants us to be happy."[1] You beam around the table. "Beer is hardly different from vegetable soup, except it doesn't have those little letters floating around in it."

"For heaven's sake," your wife mutters, so thoroughly

---

1. "Ben Franklin, Great American," W. Bruce Cameron. History 101 term paper, grade C minus.

defeated by the brilliance of your statements she has little left to say.

"And have you ever been to Kansas?" you challenge your younger daughter. She has, but so deft are you in this debate, she is afraid to admit it. "What do you suppose lives in the state of Kansas?"

No answer.

"Cows," you tell her. "Miles and miles of cows. They're taking over the planet! If we don't do something about it soon, every house in America will be overrun by cattle."

"Cool," your son breathes.

"That is the stupidest thing I have ever heard," your younger daughter declares. This is always her last resort, a scorched-earth retreat you've learned to ignore.

You slap your hands together. "Let's have steak and beer for dinner—I'm on a vegetarian diet!"

Conclusion

Despite all the energy a parent puts into feeding a teenage daughter, most of her calories are consumed outside of the home, in congregation with other ravenous teens. Even during the middle of her weight-loss frenzy, when every bite a father takes is ruined by having its fat content analyzed in mid-chew, the daughter will think nothing of devouring a peanut buster parfait at Dairy Queen. "That's with my *friends*," she'll explain when you point out the apparent conflict.

I have no idea what is happening to the food being consumed by teenagers. Certainly it isn't being converted to energy—when they've finished eating, all teenagers want to do is loll around like lions after a feast. If you try to mention that it is only fair that you get some work out of your daughters—after all, you've put a lot of money into the groceries they've just eaten—they'll pretend they don't see the connection. In their view, you *have* to feed them, no questions asked. It's your job: you're the father.

The High-Tech
Teenager

I've Seen the Future and Only Our Children Can Figure Out How It Works

Things were much more difficult when I was a teenager, something I may have previously mentioned but that I believe my children would agree bears repeating. As an example, back in those days, when we wanted to change channels on the television, we had to *get up out of the chair* to do so—no one had remote control. The first remotes to hit the market were chunky devices with only a couple of buttons, and worked so poorly that you had better luck turning off your set by heaving the thing at the TV.

Technological advances have now made it possible for the father's easy chair to be a virtual command center—with "picture in a picture," for example, I can sit there on game day and watch two beer commercials at once. Using our new cordless telephones, I can employ the handset as a walkie-talkie, joyfully informing my wife of touchdowns and other important occurrences. (Oddly, she doesn't appear very appreciative of this favor.)

When it comes to raising my children, however, I cannot think of a single instance in which technology has made my life easier. In fact, in many ways all the new devices have introduced wholly new and unexpected opportunities for stress.

"Everyone has a cell phone"

My older daughter, serving in her role as head of the Purchasing Department, submitted a requisition to the controller (me, and I love that title for the power it implies) for the purchase of a cell phone. Delivered orally, the request went something like this.

> **Purchasing:** I can't believe we don't have a cell phone. I was at a party and I was like the only person there who wasn't talking on one.
>
> **Controller:** Wait a minute, you mean you were at a party and everyone was sitting around talking on cell phones?
>
> **Purchasing:** Except *me*.
>
> **Controller:** Who were they talking to?
>
> **Purchasing:** Obviously not me, duh.
>
> **Controller:** Right, you've made that point. I'm just trying to understand what is the point of a party where everyone goes and talks on their cell phones.
>
> **Purchasing:** They were talking to their friends.
>
> **Controller:** Who were at the party, right?
>
> **Purchasing:** You are the meanest man in the world.

Controller: We will not be purchasing a cell phone. If you want to talk to your friends, ask them to hang up.

But then my wife (chief financial officer) became involved. "Maybe we should get a cell phone for the children," she suggested a few days after the absolute final decision had been made already.

"What? Are you a secret agent for the phone company or something? The only time I see our teenagers off the phone is when they're in the car, and you want to change that?"

"But what if something bad were to happen? Wouldn't you want them to be able to call?"

"If we're worried about that, we shouldn't let them leave the house," I pointed out reasonably.

"Honey, I'm just saying, I think it would be better if we had a cell phone for when they need to get in touch with us. Like the other night, the movie was sold out and your daughter didn't have a way to let us know she went ice-skating instead."

"Two words: Pay. Phone."

"They have a special plan that includes a free phone and one hundred free minutes a month," she noted seductively.

"I'm against it."

"I think we should."

Time to put my foot down. "Absolutely not."[1]

"I'll get one Monday."[2]

"Okay."

Now, I hate to embarrass my wife in these pages, so I'll be kind and say that this was yet another instance when she was horribly and completely wrong. This cell phone, a device that was supposedly going to reduce anxiety by allowing our children to contact us in the event of any problems, only increased my worries.

"Where can she be?" I fretted a few days after the arrival of the cell phone. My older daughter had taken it with her when she left that evening, but hadn't availed herself of its functions to keep me updated as the evening progressed. "This meeting of the girls' boxing team was supposed to be over by now."

"It's not a *boxing team*, for heaven's sake. It's a fund-raiser. They're going to sell boxer *shorts* with the school mascot on them. They're meeting tonight to settle on the final design," my wife chided.

"What? That's entirely inappropriate. I do not want my daughter discussing men's underwear."

"I ordered you a dozen," she replied.

---

1. When it comes to financial matters, what I say goes.
2. Not.

"A dozen! Why do I need a dozen pair of underpants with a weasel on them?"

"It's not a weasel, it's a wolf, and you know that."

"All I know is that my daughter is out late on a school night."

"It's only seven-thirty."

"Well, it's dark outside."

"I'm sure she'll be home soon," she soothed.

"I'm calling her."

"I thought you said that the cell phone was only to be used in case of an emergency?"

"This *is* an emergency, I don't know where she is!"

I impatiently dialed the number. After a few rings, my daughter answered.

"Where are you? It's almost midnight!" I demanded.

"Dad, I can't talk right now, Heather is calling me right back."

"What? The cell phone is only for emergencies."

"This *is* an emergency!" she shouted, hanging up.

When I called her right back to tell her not to use the phone, I was greeted by her voice: *"Hello, you've reached my personal voice mail,"* she said. *"If you're hearing this, it means this stupid phone my dad bought me ran out of batteries again. Leave your message and I'll call you back as soon as I recharge it."* (I didn't even know we had voice mail!)

My younger daughter's solution to the whole problem is simply to turn off the cell phone whenever she doesn't want to talk to me, which is all the time.

"I tried to reach you," I greeted her when she walked in the door one night. "The cell phone was off. Hey, come back here, I want to talk to you."

Sighing, she stopped and turned around.

"Why did you turn off the phone?"

"You said it's for emergencies. I didn't have an emergency," she explained in a deadly patient voice.

"Yes, but I needed to reach you," I pointed out.

"I didn't consider *that* to be an emergency, either."

"Next time you take the cell phone, you must leave it turned on."

"Fine, I won't take it."

"You must take it."

"I thought you were against buying it in the first place?"

"Please pay attention to the central issue here, which is that you may not turn off the cell phone when I am trying to reach you."

"Fine."

"I mean it."

"I said fine."

"I'm not going to argue with you about this."

"Good."

The next time she went out, she took the cell phone . . . and left it turned off.

When the first bill came, I was excited to see that it was far more than I had expected. Adding up the calls, I concluded it would have been cheaper to launch our own communications satellite.

I called my older daughter on the cell phone.

"Dad, I can't talk right now, I need to make a call."

I explained to her that she had turned the telephone into a device for converting our income into digital signals, and asked her to desist immediately.

"I thought we had one hundred free minutes!" she protested.

"Yes, but not a *day*," I informed her. "You need to stop calling your friends on it. It's to be used only to report in to your father."

"Hang on, someone's calling in."

"What?" I asked the empty air. After a full minute, she came back on. "Okay, sorry. Listen, I need to go."

"I didn't realize you could put me on hold and take another call, but I guess that explains how you've managed to run up more than an hour's worth of airtime in less than sixty minutes," I told her, squinting at the phone bill.

"Whatever. Bye, Dad."

"Wait!"

Fortunately, I gained an unlikely ally in my battle against airtime—my daughters' high school, which sent home a note advising me that my older daughter would have to stop bringing the cell phone into the school building. "More than once, your daughter has interrupted class with a telephone call, and doesn't seem to grasp that this is a problem for the other students," the principal wrote.

I showed the note to my older daughter, who was outraged. "Like it's my fault the phone rings," she stormed. But she began leaving the phone in its recharging cradle at home, taking it with her only at night, which led to the cell phone company sending a representative out to our house to make sure we were all right. I explained the new procedure to him, and he wasn't happy. "This will have a serious effect on our second-quarter profits," he scolded.

"PC" Stands for "Paternal Confusion"

"I need a laptop computer," my older daughter told me at dinner one evening.

"Me too, I need a laptop," my younger daughter agreed.

"Can I have a snowboard?" my son wanted to know.

"No one needs a laptop. We have a perfectly good computer in the den."

"Well, I need it for homework tonight," my older daughter claimed.

"No, I need it," my younger daughter countered.

Then they stared at me as if I were going to be fooled by this orchestrated dispute.

"When I was a teenager . . . ," I told them.

"Never mind!" they shouted.

That evening, I went in to see how my older daughter was doing on her homework. She has perfected the technique of downloading research off the Internet, and then cutting and pasting the results into a report. A little manipulation of the fonts, a nice border, and some imported art, and she can produce a world-class thesis on a subject without learning anything about it.

I peered over her shoulder. A small window was open, a steady stream of chat pouring into it.

Q: WHO HAS THE BEST BUTT, MEL GIBSON OR JEAN-CLAUDE VAN DAMME?

A: WHAT ABOUT MATTHEW MCCONAUGHEY?

A: BRAD PITT FOR SURE.

"Is this for anatomy class?" I asked.

"Dad, this is private!" she hissed. "I'm working on my homework."

"It is not private, that's a public chat room," I informed her archly.

"Now can you see why I need a laptop? I can't have people coming in here to read my private messages!"

A new window opened up. *HEY BABY! WANNA GET NAKED W/ME??!?* it greeted.

"Who's that?" I demanded.

"How should I know? Some guy I met on-line," she snapped.

"You're doing on-line *nudity*?"

"Would you please just let me get back to my homework?"

A: MEL GIBSON IS CUTE BUT TOO OLD, I was informed to my dismay. "What do you mean, too old? He's my age!" I protested.

"In your dreams, Dad," my daughter muttered, typing furiously. *CHILL I HAVE A LAM HERE*, she wrote.

"What's LAM?" I asked.

"Large albino male," she answered tersely. "It means Dad."

HOW ARE YOU DOING WITH YOUR HOMEWORK? the message scrolled in innocuous response.

NEED HELP WITH MATH, another person agreed.

"You must think I'm a DAMFOOL," I told my daughter.

She moved her lips for a second, then glanced up at me curiously. "What's that?"

"Dumb albino male who can't figure out our language," I answered, leaving the room. Sometimes it's better if you just don't know what your daughters are doing.

Now for the Fax

I went out and bought a fax machine, figuring that as a writer I would need it for six-figure contracts, Pulitzer Prize notifications, and the like. I plugged it in and it sat mutely in the corner.

"What's the fax number?" my older daughter wanted to know.

"Why?" I answered suspiciously.

"Just in case I need, like, something from school or something," she responded. I gave it to her and within ten minutes received my first fax. It was from Heather.

> Services were held today for
> local airline pilot Harold McDuff,
> who died peacefully in his sleep
> on Thursday. The rest of the
> passengers were not so fortunate.

"No more jokes," I said sternly. "The fax machine is only to be used for official business."

This led to a mad scheme wherein my older daughter's circle of friends would each read one page of the history assignment, underline the important parts, remove it from the book, and fax it to everyone else—that way no one would need to read any more than was absolutely necessary.

"Wait a minute, you're going to rip out the pages from the books? That's vandalizing!" I shouted.

"Don't worry, at the end of the year you can just say you lost it and it comes out of your book deposit," my daughter assured me. "You don't get in trouble or anything."

"But aren't you supposed to turn the book back in to get your deposit back?"

"Oh Dad, only dorks return their *textbooks*," she scoffed.

"No faxing of textbooks. No tearing pages!" I raged.

"I don't know why you got the fax machine if you don't understand how to use the technology," she sniffed.

The Personal Digital Assistant

My younger daughter, for the most part, eschews all the technological gizmos that have invaded our lives. "Technology is degrading the value of human life," she lectured us at dinner one night.

"Thank you, Ms. Unabomber," I replied, which earned me a warning look from my wife.

But she does have a PDA, a handheld device about the size of a calculator, into which she taps appointments and class notes with a small pointer. I'll watch her bent over this instrument for hours at a time, clicking away silently.

"What are you working on?" I ask.

She looks up, bringing me into focus with a frown. "Nothing."

"Nothing. For two straight hours, you've been scrawling nothing. You don't need a PDA for that, you could just draw in the air."

A shrug. And then, amazingly, a hesitant smile. "I wrote a poem."

"Really?"

"Want to read it?"

I'm not sure I've heard correctly. "Really?"

She somehow gets her gizmo to communicate with the printer in the den, and comes out, handing my wife and me each a piece of paper.

Endless Waters

River dark and
Water chill
Relentless in its suffocating message

Relentless
Relentless
Let me
Pull you down
It says
Down
Down
And drag you cold and lifeless
To the sea

Why on earth did we ever think we could be parents? Clearly we were in over our heads.

My wife gazes at the ceiling for a moment. "It has very strong imagery. Very vivid," she finally states.

What a cop-out! My daughter seems pleased with the comment, though, and I know I need to come up with something good as well. I clear my throat. "It *is* vivid," I agree lamely. Okay, no one is impressed with this. "I can almost feel the . . . the relentless, the suffocating . . . the cold, suffocating, relentless, um . . ." I look at them, feeling myself being pulled down, down, down. My brain has gone cold and lifeless trying to find something positive to say. "I'm not sure I completely understand it," I eventually admit.

My daughter collects her papers and leaves the room,

not appearing affected by my lack of literary comprehension. I shake my head as she departs, turning to my wife. "Well, that's certainly cheerful!" I gush. "Let's call Hallmark, see if they're coming out with a Despondency series anytime soon."

"Now, is that nice? She worked hard."

"The poem was about *suffocation*. Is *that* nice?"

She purses her lips. "The problem is, she uses that PDA for more than just poetry."

"What do you mean?" I say cautiously.

"The school called. Not only do they use those little palm devices to take notes in class, but apparently they can flash electronic messages to one another. The school wants to ban them, but the kids use them in their work."

My head hurts. "I never did anything like that when I was a teenager," I lament. "I just took notes."

"Your parents say you never studied at all."

"Well, I was naturally gifted and didn't need to crack the books very often."

"Your mother says it was a miracle you even graduated."

"Why do you talk to my mother?"

"Then *you* talk to her. She says you never call."

"I hate it when you argue in circles!"

"All right, so what should we do?"

I sigh. "I'll talk to her," I say. I want another shot at complimenting the poem, anyway. I get to my feet with a groan so my wife will know what a sacrifice this is—you never know when you're going to need some points to cash in with my wife.

My younger daughter is hunched over her PDA when I knock on her door. "Hey," I greet her tentatively.

She looks up, pushing her hair out of her eyes. A lot of silence builds up between us—talking to this girl used to be so *easy*.

"So let me look at that poem again," I suggest.

She doesn't respond for several seconds, just keeps writing, and I wonder if maybe I'm pushing my luck, attempting to have two conversations with her in the same night. Then she sets down her stylus and hands me the paper.

"It's about death, right?" I finally guess.

She nods solemnly, gazing at me. "When it happens, it is like a dark river, the current pulling you, but then you're out to sea, which is vast, like the universe or heaven, right?" I offer.

She nods again, a faint blush coming to her cheeks.

"It's really good," I tell her sincerely.

For just a moment, something leaps across the barriers between us. At a different time, a different age, I would have hugged her and she would have kissed me on the cheek.

"So show me how to use that gizmo," I request finally. "Can you really send messages to your friends in class?"

She demonstrated how easy it was for her to communicate with her pals, moving the little pointer across the screen with sure dexterity. "Pretty cool," I told her.

My wife was reading the paper when I walked out into the living room.

"Did you talk to her about sending notes in class?" she demanded.

"Yep," I responded truthfully.

Conclusion

I guess I would agree that cell phones have a purpose beyond the cell phone bill—without them, people driving their cars would have nothing to do except maybe concentrate on traffic. But I don't notice that allowing my daughters to speak more frequently to their friends has done anything to increase the quality of *my* days.

I also no longer insist that computers are a passing fad. They are now a part of my everyday life, enabling me to receive far more junk mail than was ever before possible, and allowing Internet publishers to grab copies of my writings and publish them without bothering me with any pesky income. But I don't believe they are necessary to the task of raising children, despite my daughters' claims that we've "absolutely got to have" a better PC so that they can download the graphics necessary to answer once and for all the question of who has the best butt in the movies.

You may have already reached the same conclusion I have about all these new devices: your kids are always going to understand them better than you are. Not long ago, my younger daughter demonstrated to me how she can use her PDA to send a message to the PC, which then somehow managed to send the same message to the text display on the cell phone. "Almost as easy as dialing the cell phone itself!" I marveled. I don't have any idea why anyone would actually want to do such a thing, and you probably don't either.

It's enough to make you long for the days when the only thing children could do with technology was break it. "Don't touch the VCR!" you'd shout, too late to stop them from stuffing a banana in it. Now they yell at you. "Dad, don't mess with the PC, I have a download going!"

By creating the illusion that you are technologically dim-witted, all these new devices have forced an unnatural state of affairs on the family, with the teenagers inappropriately lecturing you for "screwing up the operating system," whatever that means. My advice is to remind them that PCs were invented by fathers (haven't you heard the expression "the father of the personal computer"?) and therefore if anybody in the house knows how to work the infernal thing, it must be you. Stick to this story and don't change it despite their derision. You are the father.

Prohibited
Teenage
Fashions

Cloth, Paint, and Metal Turn Your Teenage Daughter into an Advertisement for Unauthorized Activities

The purpose of clothing is to cover the body, to keep it warm and out of the sight of boys. One can picture when the cavemen, or I guess we call them cavepeople now, first decided to wrap themselves in bison skins, and it probably went like this.

> **First Cave Teenage Daughter:** Look, I'm wearing the skin from yesterday's kill, what do you think?
> **Second Cave Teenage Daughter:** Well, you look like a bison.
> **First Cave Teenage Daughter:** Thank you!

It probably did *not* go like this:

> **First Cave Teenage Daughter:** Look, I'm wearing the skin from yesterday's kill, what do you think?
> **Second Cave Teenage Daughter:** I think you should shorten it to fifteen inches above the knee, and then cut slits on the sides all the way up to your rib cage. In front, scoop out a plunging neckline, and then wear something underneath that thrusts your breasts out

for every guy to ogle at. And it needs to be a lot tighter—why leave anything to the imagination?

First Cave Teenage Daughter: Good idea!

Cave Father: You are *not* leaving the house dressed like that!

No doubt it was at this moment in history that the Cave Father first heard the words, "But this is how *everybody* dresses," which is what teenage daughters still say to this day. And it's true, if you define "everybody" as your daughter's three best friends and ignore everybody else. Don't even bother pointing out to your daughter that her "everybody" sample is rather small. She will come up with an exhausting rationale for why the majority of the population is excluded from consideration. ("Oh, you can't count *her*," your daughter will sneer when you ask about a very stylish yet modestly dressed high school student. "She's in like the Ecology Club.") Instead, state very reasonably, "I don't care what everybody is wearing. Everybody is not my daughter. *You* are my daughter, and you will put on something that retains body heat, instead of causing it."

This is, sad to say, one of the duties of a father: to make sure his daughter's epidermis is tucked in at all times. It's a multifront battle, one fought not just over skimpy clothing but also over jewelry and makeup, and with surprisingly few allies—your wife, for example, will see nothing wrong with your daughter getting her ears pierced when she is *nine years old*, because it is so "cute." This is sort of like allowing Hitler to take Czechoslovakia: it does not stop there. Worse, when you suggest a compromise (you said twenty-seven years of age, she said nine, a numerical middle is eighteen), everyone will pretend you don't even have a *vote* in the matter!

Fathers are advised not to give up. Eventually the daughter will come flouncing in sporting some fashion accessory that will horrify even your wife, and you'll finally have someone on your side. (You'll be tempted, at this point, to smugly point out that you were right all along and that if everyone had listened to you in the first place, maybe your daughter wouldn't have a seven-inch chain dangling from her left nostril. I should note, though, that there's really nothing to be gained by saying this except to make your wife feel wretched, so by all means go ahead.)

Makeup: When Even a Little Is Too Much

When a little girl is a baby, she wears very sensible clothing. And if there's anything on her face, it's chocolate or ketchup. As she grows older, she'll dress in fewer sailor outfits and will stop insisting that every top she puts on sport a picture of Winnie-the-Pooh, and she may even, from time to time, smear on some sweet-smelling strawberry Chap Stick, but none of this is alarming. People's tastes change, after all, and fathers are encouraged to accept this, even if they don't fully understand it.

But then they evolve into teenagers. Their styles become all about flesh—clothes that expose it, jewelry that pierces it, and makeup that paints it.

The first hint that the easy days are over and that the dad must step in and begin dictating what his daughters put on comes in the form of stains and powders impregnating his child's skin. Fortunately, this isn't a sign that a man can miss: one day his daughter is sitting across the table from him as scrubbed and wholesome as Punky Brewster. The next morning she comes to breakfast looking like Elvira.

"Is there a costume party at school today?" you ask carefully. She blinks at you, her makeup as thick as a two-by-four.

"What do you mean?" she asks innocently, as if she has forgotten that she spent an extra half hour this morning standing at the mirror and applying what looks like purple epoxy to her face. Her view of you must be so obscured by the layers of slop she's like a soldier peering out of the gun slip of a cement pillbox in World War II.[1]

"You're wearing makeup," you reply. This is called "parental understatement" and is an indication of the level of sophistication you have attained in raising your children.

She attempts to bat her eyes demurely in response, but the lashes are so encrusted in mascara they get stuck shut. "A little," she admits, no slouch in the understatement department herself. "I went and had a makeover yesterday."

A makeover! You and your wife did a great job making her the first time, why does she think she needs to be redone? "Where did you go, the mortician's?"

"The mall," she replies in an "of course" voice.

You sense you are witnessing one of those watershed events in the relationship with your young teenage daughter, a turning point that will flavor the nature of the next half decade. There will be lots of changes ahead, and your daughter needs to have the freedom to express her individuality. You know she won't look like this every morning, because if she does the vice squad will begin tailing her around town. This is just her first faltering step toward womanhood,

---

1. When you make a reference to Hitler's invasion of Czechoslovakia and then later talk about World War II pillboxes, it's considered to be really good writing.

inexpertly executed, an attempt to master what surely must be the rather difficult task of applying subtle shades of color to her face. What's called for here is tolerance, understanding, even encouragement.

"Scrub your face or you're not leaving the house," you encourage tolerantly.

"*What?*" she shrieks. Tears spring forth and begin eroding deep gullies down her cheeks.

"You can use my putty knife if you need to, but you're not leaving the house looking like that," you continue.

Though you've been very supportive, a backlash will quickly undermine you, as the females of the family seize suffrage and vote that the father may not have any say in how much makeup may be worn, even if it is obviously too much. Your daughter will stomp out the door with a clean face for that last morning only, but her purse will be bulging with lip goo, eye black, and cheek cake, and by the time she arrives at school she'll be back to looking like Elizabeth Taylor in *Cleopatra*.

Time for you to get busy. This opening volley just signals the start of a long, protracted conflict, and the only opportunity to prepare your forces is now, while your adversaries are celebrating their victory. When your daughter returns from school, you should present her with your policies on Prohibited Fashions.

A Father's Very Reasonable Policies on Prohibited Fashions
Instructions Regarding Bras and Underwear

I understand the fact that it is now necessary for you to wear a bra. Well, this isn't completely true, since I don't really understand what a bra does, and I don't want to know! Don't tell me! I'm not asking!

At any rate, I have no problem with you wearing bras, so long as they don't mingle with my laundry and wind up being in a place where I might see them. However, you don't seem to understand the purpose of underwear. The word "under" is not in there by accident— you're supposed to keep your bra completely hidden from view by burying it in bulky clothing. Lately I've noticed that you're wearing skimpy tops that allow your bra straps to show. This is unacceptable and completely and totally prohibited. A visible bra strap is just a signal to boys that you now have breasts. They don't need to know this. I don't need to know this, either. Let's just keep it an appalling secret.

And while we're on the subject, I also cannot help but notice (due to your defective clothing, which allows your underwear to poke out or to be visible right through your garments!) that instead of the plain, no-nonsense bras you should be wearing, you're flouncing around in front of boys wearing items out of the Victoria's Secret catalogue.

Now, this puts me in something of a quandary. My official position, up until this point, has been that I have been willing to do whatever is necessary to keep those catalogues arriving at our house. I've studied the pages at great length, and have come up with several excellent ideas for what your mother should wear, which she has been ignoring for many years. Now, however, you *daughters* are buying things from that catalogue, and I don't want to know what you've bought! Don't tell me! I just want to point out that the items in that catalogue are not appropriate. I don't mind if other women want to wear them, but you may not. I'd like to suggest T-shirts from JCPenney. And how come you never wear anything with Winnie-the-Pooh anymore?

When it comes to panties, a father should *never* know what his daughters wear, but you won't let me be ignorant because every once in a while you leave a pair in the bathroom sink as if you are preparing some sort of underpants soup. In order to shave I must remove them, which I do with a kitchen utensil and an appropriately squeamish expression. During this process, I noticed you have started wearing thong underwear, completely abandoning the white cotton look that you sported so successfully for so many years.

Thong underwear is about as sensible as wearing a sling-shot. I can't imagine why anyone would voluntarily put on a wedgie, and the cost per square inch is surely prohibitive.

In my opinion, a daughter's underwear has the same purpose as the police: to preserve and protect. Please insure that from now on, every pair of panties you purchase makes good on this motto.

My Swimsuit Policy

A brief history lesson is in order. Swimming pools were originally invented as a place where people could swim. (Am I going too fast for you here?) To facilitate this athletic endeavor, swimsuits (there's that "swim" word again) were invented.

Your information about what to wear at the pool seems to have come from *Sports Illustrated*. I'd invite you to take a close look at the women in those pictures—I know I certainly have. What do you see? That's right, none of them are actually *swimming*. That's because if they were to dive into the water, what little they are wearing would wash right off.

The bathing suit you brought home to wear this summer is good only for strolling around the pool and igniting boys. This is a prohibited activity.

You may wear the thing, but only if you wear a T-shirt underneath. That is my reasonable policy on swimsuits.

A Few Thoughts on Shoes

The purpose of shoes is not to add altitude so that you wind up looking like you're trying out for a role in *Land of the Giants*. Here's a tip: if you find yourself taller than Dikembe Mtumbo, you are wearing the wrong shoes. Instead of the ten inches of leather you've put between yourself and the planet Earth, why not try buying something with material on *top* of your feet, so we don't have to see that you've painted each of your toenails a different color?

The heels you wear look like they were designed by the Society for the Promotion of Ankle Sprain. Watching you wobble atop your rickety platforms, I understand why you want me to buy you a car—you're certainly not going to be able to *walk* anywhere.

Some Guiding Principles on Body Piercing

Body piercing is the act of having small holes drilled into your flesh and then filling those holes with metal. It makes a teenager's face as attractive as studded snow tires. One need only watch a bass-fishing show on television to realize where the inspiration for body piercing came from—though for the fish, the silver hook in its lip may not be considered a fashion accessory.

> **Male Fish:** Say, I notice you've gone in for some treble-hooked lip piercing, there.
> **Female Fish:** Yes, I saw it moving past at a constant speed and just had to snap it up. Do you like it?
> **Male Fish:** Very attractive!
> **Female Fish:** Oops, I'm being reeled in. Gotta go!

Unlike clothing, body piercing is not something you can bring into compliance with the father's reasonable rules by simply adding more of it. It requires its own very reasonable policy: *You may have yourself punched full of holes the day you've put me in a box and lowered me into the ground. Until then, I'm going to assume that any metal protruding from your lips or eyelids is there because you attempted to eat a worm dangling at the end of a line of monofilament, and I will use my hook extractor to remove it.*

Of Skirts, Pants, and Blouses

We do not live in Bora Bora. You must cover yourself adequately so you don't catch a cold or a boyfriend.

Clothing should be loose enough to allow a certain amount of movement. Sometimes the outfits you put on are so constrictive I get a crushing sensation in my chest.

My very reasonable policy on skirts, pants, and blouses is that they shouldn't flunk the "too" rule. That is, they shouldn't be too tight, too short, too revealing, too skimpy, too clingy, or too see-through. To find out if something flunks the "too" rule, you need only ask me.

A Morning's Mad Dash to School

Despite the fact that school occurs on a regular basis, with the well-known departure time of 7 A.M. formally promulgated each night by my wife, my children react with complete shock, anger, and confusion when they suddenly realize, usually at about 6:45, that they are going to have to get dressed and go to school.

My wife and I have, over the years, perfected a system of divided responsibility when it comes to parental support of the morning's preparations. I'm in charge of current events, carefully reading the paper and calling out facts to the rest of the family, while my wife assists the children in getting dressed. (You'd think they could handle this task on their own, but somehow it all becomes one giant family project.)

On occasion, and despite my stern instructions that it never be allowed to happen, my wife will have an early meeting, sneaking out of the house before I'm even awake. *I set some chicken out to thaw,* her note reads. *Do not take it with you this morning. It is NOT your lunch.*

Okay, look, that happened *once*. I don't know why she brings this up all the time.

Your son is still on bus probation for throwing orange peels out the window, so you'll have to drive him. Do not forget and leave him at home!

Again, one time, maybe twice, did this happen. This woman can really carry a grudge.

I love you! the note concludes. That's very sweet, but it doesn't change the fact that the delicate division of labor around the house has been upset by her early departure.

My son's philosophical stance is that education is an optional activity, with little appeal or value to him personally. He apparently doesn't see the need to get out of bed prior to his actual departure, so one of the challenges every morning is to make sure he is part of the team.

"It's six-thirty!" I shout in the general direction of my children's bedrooms. "Is everybody awake?"

There is no reply. Reluctantly, I trudge down the hallway. I pound on my older daughter's door. "Are you awake? Hello?"

"What?" Her voice sounds like it is filtered through sandpaper.

"Are you awake in there?" I attempt to open the door, but the heap of dirty laundry on the other side makes such efforts futile.

"What time is it?" she rasps from inside her tomb.

"It's six-thirty! You mean you aren't up yet?"

"What day is it?"

"It's Monday!"

There's a pause while she digests this unfortunate bit of news. "Do we have school today?"

"Yes! Get out of bed, you're running late!"

My son's body is as responsive as a frozen fish when I shout at it, but after repeated shakings, he opens an eye and regards me as if I am a perfect stranger. "Time to get up," I urge.

"Is it a snow day?" he asks hopefully.

"Just get out of bed."

"What time is it?"

News of the invention of watches and alarm clocks has apparently failed to reach my children. "It's six-thirty-two," I report.

"Oh." He rolls over. "Half an hour," he mumbles.

"No, get out of bed now!" I thunder.

At my younger daughter's door, light streams from

underneath, though when I knock there is no indication of life on the other side. I pound and it eventually swings open; a small set of headphones is draped on her neck like a stethoscope. "What?" she demands.

"I just wanted to make sure you were awake," I say cheerfully, heartened to see that she is already dressed.

"I don't need you to wake me up," she responds coldly, shutting the door.

Six-forty. I wander back down the hallway. "We're running late!" I announce. This is our Official Family Motto.

My older daughter yanks open her door. She is wearing her hair in a towel and has thick green goop smeared on her face, as if someone has hit her in the face with an avocado cream pie. It's rather frightening. "I have to print my report on the causes of the Civil War!" she screams at me.

"You might also consider scraping the ooze off your face," I suggest. "It looks like it is becoming gangrenous."

"Can you print it for me? Here's the disk!" She flings a floppy at me and slams her door without waiting for an answer.

Okay, I'll do it, I say to myself. I turn on the computer. My son stumbles out, a study in lethargy. He falls to the couch, collapsing as if his nervous system has short-circuited. "Get up!" I tell him. "Eat breakfast! Get dressed!

Feed the dog!" He blinks, attempting to process all of these commands. "Go!" I shout.

He goes, leaving the room in the direction of the kitchen. I have no confidence he will be able to accomplish anything once he is there.

My daughter's essay on the Civil War blames the Confederate shelling of Fort Sumter as the sole reason for the conflict. "Hey," I shout at her. "Don't you think there were more causes than this? Like, I don't know, slavery?"

She opens her door. The green stuff is gone from her face, but her hair is still wrapped in a towel. "Fort Sumter's what our teacher said caused it!" she hisses at me.

"I'm sure what he said was that this was the immediate provocation that started the fighting, but the root causes were much more complex," I explain pontifically.

"Well, fine. You just call the principal and tell him that my history teacher doesn't know what he is talking about, then!" she snaps.

"That's not what I am trying to say," I protest. "The real fighting started at Sumter, but that's not the reason America fought the war."

"Well, maybe when you were in school the cause was different! I don't care, I don't have time to put in your old-fashioned ideas! It was due Friday!"

"Friday? You mean to tell me you wait until Monday to print a report that was due last Friday?"

"Well, maybe if you would just let me write what the teacher tells me I could get it in on time!" she shrieks.

I cannot think of a reply that doesn't include raving. Gritting my teeth, I click on the print button.

It's five minutes of seven. My younger daughter emerges from her room, wearing black pants, a black T-shirt, and a black sweater. "Are you going to a coven meeting after school?" I ask her. She rolls her eyes and walks into the kitchen.

Breakfast consists of accusations and threats. Apparently no one is willing to pass the milk or the cereal. "Can we order this, Dad?" my son asks, pointing to the back of the cereal box: *2,000-Volt Death Ray!* reads the ad. *Batteries not included.* "No, son," I tell him, "we've exceeded our quota of toys with the word 'death' in them for this year."

The scheduled departure time of 7 A.M. passes with no apparent significance to my children. My oldest dashes in, still wearing her bathrobe. "Can you fix me a bagel?" she pleads. "And I need money for lunch."

"I need money for lunch!" my son chimes.

"I need money for lunch," my younger daughter agrees.

"Why don't we ever make lunch?" I ask. "That might save money. Money is our friend."

"Only complete dorks take their own lunch," my younger daughter sneers.

"I *always* made my own lunch," I counter airily. She gives me a you-just-proved-my-point expression.

"We're running late," I announce.

"Dad, if we had a great white shark, what would we feed it?" my son wants to know.

"Could you just finish your breakfast? And brush your teeth," I tell him.

"I have nothing to wear!" my oldest child screams from down the hallway.

This cannot possibly be true. There's enough clothing on the floor of her bedroom to outfit the entire twelfth grade. "We're running late!" I tell her helpfully.

My son has decided to train the dog to climb up on the table and lick out of the cereal bowl. "Get down!" I command. The dog gives me a hurt expression. "Is that what you are wearing?" I ask of my son. He's clothed in a flannel shirt and a pair of pants with a ludicrous number of pockets. "Sure," he says.

"Isn't that what you slept in?" I demand.

"Sure," he says.

Well, what the heck.

My older daughter bounces back into the room. She is

sporting a skirt so short it makes my eyes water. "You're not wearing that to school," I inform her.

"Why not? It's my new skirt!"

"Because I can see your underpants, for heaven's sake," I tell her.

"You are the meanest man in the whole world," she seethes, stomping back down the hallway. When her door slams I can hear pictures falling off the walls all over the house.

"I can't believe you said that to her," my other daughter scolds me.

"Why not? It's true!"

"That's why you shouldn't have said anything," she hisses, standing up and gathering her books. "I'm getting a ride from Zero."

"From what?"

On cue, what appears to be a getaway car squeals into the driveway. The vibrations from its stereo begin rattling the front picture window. "Zero. He's a friend."

"His name is Zero?" I sputter. "His parents couldn't pick a better number than *that*?"

My younger daughter is out the door without looking back.

"This skirt is the only thing I have to put on. I'm not

wearing anything else," my other daughter declares haughtily—the teenager equivalent of firing on Fort Sumter. Perhaps to keep boys from looking up her legs, she has donned a suffocatingly tight blouse that fails to close the distance between her rib cage and her belly button.

"Put on more cloth," I tell her.

I pick up the phone and dial. *"This is the school attendance line. To report an absence, press one. To report tardiness, press two. If you are the Camerons calling to report you'll be late again, press three."*

"We're running late!" I shout.

"I have nothing else to wear!" she yells.

"Time to go!" I threaten. "Son, did you feed the dog?"

"I let her finish my cereal," he advises.

My daughter reenters the kitchen, avoiding my eyes. She has slipped on a pair of blue jeans as tight as the skin on a hot dog. Her blouse is the same inadequate specimen. "Can you expose less stomach?" I ask.

"This is the only shirt I have," she snarls.

We pack ourselves off to the car, where the children entertain themselves by fighting over what to listen to on the radio. First I drop off my daughter, who slips out of the car when it has barely stopped and slams the door as if conducting an experiment in metal fatigue. A group of squealing friends rush up to inform her of some new scandal, and I see that they are all showing stomach patches above the belt line. Perhaps the boys in school will become confused by this mass display of flesh, like cheetahs confronted with the scrambled lines of a herd of darting zebras. I hope so, anyway.

Conclusion

Clothing is not supposed to be a provocation, it is supposed to be a protection from the elements. One of those elements is boys, so when clothing proves inadequate to the job, the father must step in instead.

Makeup, on the other hand, has no purpose but accentuation. What is accentuated is the fact that your little girl may be ready to take the first big step into womanhood. Since *you* aren't ready, you must do your best to mute the impact of the paints and stains your daughter uses. And jewelry should always be (*a*) tasteful, (*b*) purchased without financial impact on the father, and (*c*) removable without leaving behind a permanent scar.

As I've noted, most of the people in the family will behave in a most inappropriately derisive fashion when the father begins laying down the law on these matters, pretending that the father's sartorial choices give him no voice in the decision. Hey, you should tell them, no one ever stares at *me* when I walk out of the house—apparently my own apparel is doing the job it was intended to do. (Not that girls will listen to this—it's almost as if they *want* to be stared at.)

Fathers don't understand why their daughters rebel against reasonable rules on fashions. Haven't you been there since the beginning, providing instructions in this area? "Honey, put on your coat, it's cold outside," you said. "No, you can't wear your ballet outfit to school." Now, after shepherding her safely through the first dozen years, you're supposed to abdicate responsibility? How is that reasonable?

Look, people are always telling you what to wear. "Your tie doesn't go with that shirt," your wife will say as you're pulling out of the driveway. So there is nothing inconsistent with you providing the same sort of advice to your teenage daughters. No one else seems willing to do it, so it's up to you. You're the father.

It's Her Party
and I'll Cry
If I Want To

Teenagers Gather Together for the Express Purpose of Violating Their Fathers' Wishes

Even though your daughters spend hours and hours with their fellow teenagers at school and at the mall, they crave even more contact—they want to initiate potentially catastrophic events known as "parties."

Teenage parties come in two flavors:

1. Unauthorized affairs organized by the kids themselves. Without any adult supervision, the kids behave inappropriately. These parties are strictly prohibited.

2. Organized, chaperoned affairs planned and managed by adults and held in safe, supervised environments. These parties are strictly prohibited too.

When Your Daughter Wants To Have A Party

As if she hasn't been paying any attention at all to what you have been saying, your daughter may approach you at some point and ask if she can throw a party herself. You might be tempted to allow this: after all, under your roof, subject to your rules and your security procedures, a party stands little chance of getting out of control, right? Well, this is like saying you can control a school of piranhas after a leg of lamb hits the water. Short of spraying them with a fire extinguisher, nothing can suppress the hyper-activity of a group of teenagers getting together in order to have "fun."

You may not even be asked. Teenage parties, like shower fungus, can spring up unbidden if you're not careful. First a few of your daughter's girlfriends show up. Then a boy or two appears at the door. Next thing you know, they are listening to music and ordering pizza—a party under your very own roof!

Worse yet, a simple out-of-town trip with your wife is nothing but an open invitation to all the teenagers in the four-county area to come to your house and destroy your belongings. As you leave, handing your daughters a list of chores to perform while you are gone, their faces look so scrubbed and innocent you are lulled into a sense of com-plete security, unaware that at that very moment the local radio station is running ads for the riot to be held at your house that night.

Five Signs Your Daughter Had a Party While You Were Out of Town

1. There are parts of your house you cannot enter because they are still cordoned off with police tape.

2. You receive a notice from the local carpet cleaners that your "next rental is completely free"!

3. Heather comes by and rather breathlessly asks if she can "check something" in your bedroom for just a minute.

4. Your next-door neighbor suddenly refuses to talk to you "on advice of my attorney."

5. The channel 9 news copter now cruises over your house once a day as part of its regular route.

The High School Dance— A True Story

The principal of my daughters' high school is an affable, even gentle man, completely the opposite of the escaped war criminal who maintained discipline when I was in high school. I even see their principal from time to time outside of school, at social occasions and at the hardware store—

my high school principal went home to sleep upside down in a closet with his wings over his face.

One day I was storming up and down the grocery store aisles, attempting to find the items my wife had listed for me, when I literally ran into the principal with my cart. I apologized and asked him where to find cumin and also what was it, and in the course of chatting, he mentioned he was short of chaperons for the high school dance that night.

"I know you don't like to do things like this, but would you be willing to chaperon tonight?" he asked me hesitantly, watching me eye the items in his cart to see if he'd located anything else I was looking for. He appeared to be much better at this whole shopping thing than I, and I found myself a little envious.

"Why do you say I don't like to do things like that?" I asked idly.

"Well, because every year both of your daughters return the parent volunteer form, and you've always checked 'not interested' when it comes to chaperoning."

"Oh really," I responded mildly, giving him my "I've never even *heard* of such a form" expression. "So every year it gets turned in by my daughters, you say."

"That's right."

I told him I would be delighted to chaperon the high school dance that night. I neglected to inform my daughters, who were already trying on inappropriate outfits when I came home.

"Do you think this is sheer enough? I want to appear nearly naked," I could picture them saying.

I arrived at the gym before the girls, feeling absurdly nervous. A group of adults beckoned me over. "Look," the principal was saying, "I don't want any heroics tonight. If the boys start a fight, call security. Nobody goes in and tries to break it up."

"What if there is kissing?" I wanted to know.

The principal shrugged. "We really can't stop that."

"I mean kissing on the lips."

"Right."

"Between a boy and a girl, I mean."

"I understand, Mr. Cameron. We really can't stop that."

"I mean, what if my daughters do it?"

The adults all laughed as if I had told a joke. I frowned at the inadequacy of my fellow chaperons. Clearly it would be up to me to put a stop to all unacceptable behavior.

We paired off, the rookies partnered with more-seasoned veterans. I found myself working with Miss DeKeyser, a biology teacher who had been described to me by my daughters variously as a "spinster" and "an old lady who never got married and now it is too late."

She was thirty.

As if on signal, kids began pouring through the doors. I stood with Miss DeKeyser on the staircase landing overlooking the lobby that separated the gymnasium from the academic wing, there to block any kids who attempted to access any other part of the school.

Quickly the social systems established themselves. One group of boys peeled off and sat along the wall of the lobby, concentrating on handheld video games. They never even looked up, as if mere eye contact with a girl would cause them to suffer a general protection fault.

Another group of boys knotted in a more boisterous gathering just inside the school entrance, pushing at one another and laughing loudly. From the safety of their circle they called out to the girls walking by, who blushed and chewed nervously on their necklaces.

The girls formed impregnable huddles in the center of the lobby and talked earnestly about whatever they had been discussing on the telephone all day. They looked like a herd of water buffalo forming a protective circle against predators.[1]

1. Look, I'm not saying anybody's daughter looks like a buffalo. I'm just saying their *behavior* reminds me of a TV program I saw about how these huge four-legged creatures would form a circle, horns out, to ward off lions and other bison stalkers.

When my wife reads this I know she's going to be angry. "Why would you call them water buffalo?" she'll want to know. "What am I supposed to say to Heather's mother? Why couldn't you have picked a more graceful animal, like a gazelle?"

Well, sorry, but there were no gazelles in the show. I can't be expected to watch every documentary that comes on television just so I won't hurt Heather's feelings.

And there *were* predators, lone wolves hungrily circling amongst the herds, probing for weaknesses. At this point, the defenses appeared strong, but I knew as the night grew long that the tightly knit social fabric of each group of girls would begin to fray, leaving the ones on the perimeter vulnerable to attack.

"Why did they even bother to decorate the gym if they're all going to mill around out here?" I asked Miss DeKeyser.

"They'll drift in when the music starts," she predicted.

I spotted my daughters, who came in the front door and immediately separated, as if the ride to the school had been more exposure than they could endure. My older daughter went over to her clan, which was gathered in the very center of the lobby so that everyone would be able to see them ignoring everybody else. They greeted my child with loud cries of joy, as if she were returning from discovering China. They swooned over her dress and demanded to see her earrings. They even hugged: it is for behavior like this that the word "ridiculous" was coined.

My younger daughter found her friends hanging out in the hall outside the gym, slouched tiredly against the wall, and went to join them in sullen communion. They registered her arrival with the faintest of reactions, a slight, creaking adjustment in their pouty features. Clearly, they had a pact with one another not to enjoy themselves at this party under any circumstances.

I told Miss DeKeyser I would be right back and wandered downstairs to say hello.

When my oldest saw me, her eyes bulged. She instantly broke from the herd, which fell into a pensive silence as she stormed over to me.

"What are you doing here?" she hissed, trying to talk to me without moving her lips.

"I'm a chaperon."

"A *what*?"

"You know, like on that form I fill out every year?"

She peered around the room. "Dad, you have to leave *right now*. All of my friends are here."

"Oh good, why don't you introduce me?"

"No! Why are you doing this to me? You're ruining everything!"

"I don't recognize everyone over there—well, except Heather, and she's always crying when I see her because she and Burke broke up."

She stared at me. "How can you be so cruel? Heather and Burke just broke up this afternoon. She's devastated."

"Oh for Pete's sake."

"Dad, if you don't leave right this minute, I will never speak to you again in my whole life, I swear."

"How are you going to ask for money if you don't speak to me?"

"Dad!"

"Why is it so embarrassing for your friends to see me? Did you tell them your father was Warren Beatty or something?"

"Who?"

I eventually agreed, for the sake of my daughter's social standing, that I would not go over and introduce myself as her father. I would not talk to my daughter during the course of the evening, or say hello to Heather, or make eye contact with any of her friends. I would attempt to remain as inconspicuous as possible. If anyone were to ask, I was to deny that I had ever even met my daughter.

My younger teenage daughter was still propped up against the wall. She rolled her eyes when she saw me approach, but didn't try to flee.

"Hi."

"So you're a chaperon," she stated.

"Right, it should be fun!"

"This party sucks."

I wasn't sure what to say to this.

"Why don't you go into the gym?" I suggested.

She rolled her eyes at me. Clearly, I didn't understand. I shrugged and went over to join Miss DeKeyser.

The band cranked up, and people finally began to flow into the gym from the crowded lobby. The style of music it played seemed to be a cross between hard rock and extra loud. Miss DeKeyser and I were reduced to smiling and nodding mutely at each other.

I discovered that I had a natural ability for what I came to think of as a "chaperon frown." When a girl and a boy came off the dance floor and ducked under the stairs in the entrance, I went over and frowned at them and they immediately broke from their clench. Delighted, I went into the men's room and applied frown to the boys smoking in there, who tossed down their cigarettes and hurried out.

"I'm having fun!" I shouted at Miss DeKeyser, who smiled and nodded, not hearing a word.

Heather began dancing with Burke, sending a palpable wave of relief through my daughter's friends. Their guard thus relaxed, they were unprepared for a coordinated assault from a small pack of boys, who descended and neatly split the herd in two. I sucked in my breath in horror as I saw my older daughter, alone and defenseless, turn to face a sudden attack from a lone wolf who had sensed opportunity and come loping across the room. I opened my mouth to shout a warning, but realized I would never be heard over the racket the band was making.

She never even had time to struggle. After a few brief moments, she was whisked off to the dance floor, the rest of the ungulates so obtuse they never even noticed her departure.

At the end of the "song," I waited expectantly at the side of the gym, but there was no sign of her. The music cranked up again, something called "Ode to Electrocution." A lot of energy poured out on the dance floor, with the girls all dancing in an inappropriately provocative manner.

Miss DeKeyser had found someone to stand sentry on the staircase, and now joined me. "I have both of your daughters in my classes," she yelled at me. "They're very nice girls. Very conscientious."

I shook my head. "I'm Bruce Cameron!" I yelled back, hoping she wouldn't be too embarrassed by her misidentification. She just nodded.

Another song, this one quieter and slow. I glanced frantically around the dance floor, finally locating my daughter in a dark corner. She and the boy who had abducted her appeared to be holding each other up. "Be right back," I promised the biology teacher.

I drifted over to the corner, pretending to notice my daughter as if by accident. The glare she gave me over the boy's shoulder would burn a hole in asbestos. I attempted to give her a dose of chaperon frown, but it just glanced off her. She pulled her dancing partner in a circle, so that her back was to me.

This was getting me nowhere. I loitered for a moment, hoping to break up the clench with sheer paternal propinquity, but I was fighting too potent a magnetism.

Time for stronger measures. The band cranked up a faster beat and I went back to Miss DeKeyser. "Would you care to dance?" I asked her. She laughed and nodded, and I led her by coincidence over near where my daughter was still clinging to the boy.

I'm something of a natural dancer, who can move with the music no matter what the style, even if it sounds like the band is systematically destroying its guitars. I began making up steps, which I have always found to be the most effective technique, flinging my arms around and, frankly, enjoying myself.

My pleasure increased immeasurably when my daughter finally caught sight of me. She stopped dead, her face slack with horror. Yes, it's me, your father, dancing with a biology teacher. Maybe next I'll pick math or American history.

She glanced around the gym and I followed her eyes. "Hey, Heather! Hi!" I shouted, improvising a "Hello, Heather" dance step right on the spot. Heather also stopped, giving me a chaperon frown.

Without warning, my daughter fled the dance floor, leaving her "date" looking wonderfully perplexed. He met my eyes and I shrugged, giving him a man-to-man expression that clearly said, "Well, that's women for you. You'll never understand her. And, you'll never see her again. You're better off forgetting all about her and finding some other guy's daughter to grope."

When the song ended Miss DeKeyser suggested that we go sit down because I was apparently sliding into cardiac arrest. There was no sign of my daughters—later I was to find that they were forced to convene an emergency session of the Cameron Girls, debating my behavior and eventually reaching a unanimous conclusion that they needed to flee the scene immediately.

Sitting there, contemplating how effortlessly I had extracted my daughter from danger, I realized I had inadvertently invented a new punishment, a humiliation so severe that it far outranked grounding or denial of phone privileges. If either one of my daughters ever again disobeyed me, I wouldn't have to send them to their rooms or confiscate the car keys. All I had to do was threaten to attend another one of their parties and dance with the biology teacher.

Conclusion

My wife often asks me what I "have against" teenage parties, which she describes to me as "natural." Tornadoes are natural, I point out in response; does that make them a good thing? Forest fires are natural. So are volcanic eruptions and traffic jams. Just because something is natural doesn't mean we shouldn't prevent it from happening.

Parties are like particle accelerators, taking excited molecules and bringing them together to form quarks or, even worse, babies. Ask a nuclear physicist if you doubt what I am saying.

Your daughters do not need to be made any more excited than they already are. They do not need to meet or dance with boy particles.

My advice: as soon as your daughter starts coming home from parties without a funny hat and party favors based on cartoon characters, prohibit her from attending any more. It's your responsibility to make sure she's not exposed to more fun than necessary. You're the father.

Learning
to Drive

A Chapter for Those Who Think You Lose More Sleep with a New Baby in the House Than with a Teenager Out in Your Car

Even though they've never had a telethon about it, something tragic happens to your child's legs when she becomes a teenager, rendering them incapable of their primary purpose of ambulation. Initial symptoms of this debilitating syndrome include a strident demand that she be transported to the library, the sporting event, and next door to the neighbor's house, followed closely by a request that she be taught to drive. In its final stages, the syndrome manifests itself as a demand that the father buy his daughter a car.

Most states allow teenagers to possess a learner's permit sometime before the age of sixteen. A learner's permit is a legal document that allows a teenager to terrorize a parent without fear of prosecution.

Fathers often feel they are best qualified to teach their daughters to drive, but they are wrong. Fathers should never try to teach their daughters to drive, because fathers care too much about (*a*) their cars and (*b*) their lives.

Why do teenage daughters need to learn to drive in the first place? Driving just means they have the capability of going places you don't want them to go. And surely if your daughter hasn't mastered the challenge of picking up her room, controlling a couple of thousand pounds of rolling steel is well beyond her capabilities. My advice is to keep your teenage daughter within earshot, because the teenage years are a difficult time, when a father's continual instructions are essential to keep behavior within appropriate boundaries.

If you need more convincing, allow me to tell you what happened when (before I knew better) I attempted to teach my older daughter how to drive.

A True Story of Physical Danger

In a ridiculous lapse of judgment, the state legislature where I live has decided that fifteen and a half years is old enough to get behind the wheel of a machine capable of more than a ton of momentum and aim it at other people. The law also requires that an adult be sitting next to the new driver, screaming in fear. (This last part isn't mandated by statute, but seems appropriate under the circumstances.)

When my oldest's fifteen-and-a-half "birthday" rolled around, she jumped out of bed early, showered, dressed, and didn't go to school. Gradually I became aware of her on the other side of my newspaper, tapping her fingers impatiently on the table. I frowned and she gave me a dazzling smile. "Ready to go?" she asked brightly.

Apparently Learner's Permit Day is a national holiday. "Don't you have school?" I asked.

"Today? I get my learner's permit today," she explained.

"You're not skipping school just to get a learner's permit," I objected.

This resulted in a five-minute period of hysterical raving that translated into something like "Oh yes I am." Reference was made to all of her friends, whose fathers apparently loved *them* enough to let them skip school to get *their* permits, as well as to the allegation that I had *promised* I would take her (what I said was, "We'll see") and that "Mom said I could," unverifiable because my wife was, at that moment, en route to a meeting.

Measuring the emotion pouring at me over the breakfast table, I decided I could either surrender on this point or be assaulted in a similar fashion every morning for the rest of the week. Sighing, I set down my coffee cup and agreed that yes, I would take her down to the DMV. This merited a gleeful squeal and a quick kiss on the cheek—there was a time, I recalled a bit sadly, when my daughter kissed me just for being her dad. I didn't have to *earn* it.

I did decide to turn the situation to my advantage, though—one of the tricks you learn as the father of teenage daughters.

"Before we go, you have to pick up your room."

"*What?*"

I could imagine what she was thinking: it would take a crew of four housekeepers seventy-two hours to clean up that mess. I turned back to my paper. "That's what I said."

Fifteen minutes later, she was ready to go. A skeptical inspection of her room revealed she somehow had managed to scoop up all of the junk that littered her floor and put it away. I was impressed, and told her so. (It was only that weekend that I discovered she had packed everything in suitcases and stored it in the attic.)

Though the subjects of biology, history, English, and math had always seemed like too much of a bother for her, my daughter had spent countless hours poring over the state driving handbook, and was bubbling over with information as we drove to the driver's license bureau. "If you have an object such as a ladder protruding more than five feet from the back of the car, you are required by law to tie a red flag to it," she advised, as if we were having a normal conversation. "When approaching a herd of cattle in the road, one must come to a complete stop. When pulling off the road, pull completely off, so that your left tires are more than sixteen statutory inches from the flow of traffic."

"When your teenager won't shut up, tie a red flag over her mouth and set her loose in a herd of cattle," I commented. She laughed with the sort of manic joy that can only be experienced by the truly psychotic.

At the Motor Vehicle Bureau, I seemed to be the only person to see an omen in the fact that they asked my daughter if she wanted to be an organ donor. What sort of question is that to ask with the father standing right there, already so laden with doubt he looks like he arrived wearing shackles? (They didn't ask *me* if I wanted to be an organ donor, even though I'd be riding in the car with the cause of the donation. Perhaps they figured all of my organs would be too stressed to be of use to anyone.)

My daughter took her written test and apparently passed—maybe there were a lot of questions relating to tying red flags on things. She was given a learner's permit, a piece of plastic with her picture and the words "WOE UNTO YOUR PARENTS" on it. She skipped to the car and slid in behind the driver's seat.

"Whoa, what are you doing?" I demanded.

"I'm driving!"

"No, you're riding. I'm driving."

"But I have a learner's permit!"

"And I have a brain. We're not going to make your first lesson 'How to merge into heavy traffic.' If we do that, your second lesson will be 'How to call an ambulance.' Let's drive back to the neighborhood, and you can have your first car accident there, where the speed limits are lower."

She crossed her arms and sat frowning all the way home, but brightened as we turned into our subdivision. "Now?" she asked.

"Okay," I sighed. We got out of the car, walked around the back, and collided with each other as we made our way to the opposite doors. She giggled, but I took this as yet another ominous sign. I glanced up at the sky, where vultures circled patiently.

"Okay," I said, putting on my seat belt and taking a deep breath, "we're in park."

"I know."

"Put your foot on the brake . . ."

"I know."

"And carefully move the gear shift to *D*. That stands for 'drive.'"

"I know."

"Slowly press the accelerator. I said *slowly* . . . slow down! Stop! Stop!"

"Would you just let me drive? You're making me crash," she snapped.

I carefully moved my head to make sure that the rapid application of G-forces hadn't fractured any vertebrae. We'd moved eight feet, administering a glancing blow to a neighbor's empty trash container before screeching to a halt. I sighed, wondering if there was a way to inflate the air bag *now*, just as an extra precaution.

"You started off a little too fast," I told her.

"I know it!"

"Well, can you please drive more slowly?"

Sullenly, she put the car in gear. Apparently it was very insulting to imply that after four seconds of driving she wasn't an expert at this whole process. "That's it," I encouraged. We were moving in a reasonably straight line, with our turn coming up ahead. "Okay, up here, we're going to want to slow. Put on your blinker and turn right. Okay, put on your blinker. Slow down, honey. Slow down. Are you . . . Stop! Stop!"

Flashing pains drew my attention to my right foot, which was pressed so hard against the floorboards I was in danger of punching through to the engine compartment.

"You were taking the corner a little too fast," I told her patiently.

"Well, that was no reason to yell at me!" she snarled.

"The reason I yelled was I became concerned when we drove up on the Goldsteins' lawn that you were going to hit their front porch."

"It wasn't my fault!"

"Right, the yard leaped out in front of you." Sarcasm, thy name is father.

"If you hadn't been yelling, I would have been all right."

"Okay. Let's just take it a little more easily. We've got a nice long and straight street ahead of us now. Let's get over to our side of the road, and proceed with caution," I suggested, wiping the sweat from my brow. I waved at Mrs. Goldstein, who stood watching from her front window, probably wondering why we were cruising around her lawn.

For more than a minute we proceeded without incident, and gradually I began unlocking the tension that had taken residence in every single muscle of my body.

"Here comes a car," she announced suddenly, focused on an approaching automobile. Her voice had the wavering strain characteristic of people who have noticed they are being stalked by a grizzly bear.

"That's okay," I reassured her, deliberately lifting my hand off of the door handle so I wouldn't be tempted to leap out of the car. "See how wide the street is? Let's just get over a little to give him some room. Honey, move over a little. Get out of the middle of the street. Move over. Get over! Okay, too far! Too far! Stop! Stop!"

We lurched to a halt. "Let's just sit here for a moment until I am no longer in fibrillation," I suggested.

"That wasn't my fault. Why do people have their trash cans out today anyway?"

"Perhaps—and this is just a theory—but perhaps because it's trash day."

"Stop yelling at me, it wasn't my fault. You keep saying to stop! How am I supposed to learn how to drive when you keep telling me to stop!"

"Stopping is part of driving. In fact, after riding with you today, I'd say it's the most important *part* of driving."

She crossed her arms and looked away.

"Shall we call an end to today's exercise in hysteria?"

"No, I just want to drive without you saying anything."

"Even condemned prisoners get a last statement before they're executed," I pointed out. We sat for a while in silence. "Okay, do you know what you did wrong?"

"Nothing!" she snapped.

"Well, for one thing, you got driving a little fast there."

"I was going under the speed limit," she hissed.

"True, but you generally should be moving more slowly when you are off-roading through people's yards."

"Can we just go?"

"Okay. Put the car in drive and let's go nail some more trash cans."

She gave me a scathing look before dropping the car in gear and easing forward. The rest of the ride passed without incident, and when we came to rest in our driveway I slid out on unsteady legs.

She watched me kissing the ground with her hands on her hips. "Very funny," she observed.

Leave It to Professionals

Ultimately, it occurs to you that there is no logical reason for you to be the one who sits next to your daughter while she plays "bowling for trash cans." There are driver's training schools available, where trained professionals with nerves of steel expose their cars to collision on a daily basis.

After my daughter completed her four-week course at Big Al's Driving School and Tooth-Whitening Emporium, I agreed to take a ride with her to gauge her progress.

"Progress," it seems, is a relative term. Certainly my daughter had learned to drive *faster*, flying through the neighborhood as if we were fleeing a crime scene. Several times I patiently screamed for her to slow down, and we hadn't gone half a block before I was begging to be allowed out of the car.

Big Al had taught her several things I didn't know. For

example, I was intrigued to discover that for all these years I had been misapplying the brake whenever I felt confronted with a dangerous situation, such as a car pulling out into the street in front of me. Apparently the new thinking is that a car's horn makes for a much wiser alternative. In fact, with liberal application of the horn, the brakes become utterly superfluous and will probably go the way of the hand crank.

My daughter also demonstrated to me that the foot traffic on the sidewalk is far more relevant than is the flow of automobiles in the street. When she spots a group of boys, she immediately puts the car on autopilot, craning her neck, honking, and waving at them while the vehicle in which we are traveling continues in whatever random drift it decides.

More news: red means stop, green means go, and yellow means "floor it." When the car up ahead doesn't cooperate by gunning its own engine to run the (now red) light in front of you, you can always use the horn. The brake is to be utilized only if all other alternatives, including running over pedestrians, have been attempted.

The accelerator has a single setting: mashed flat against the floorboards. This allows my daughter to peel away from stoplights and charge full tilt down the road to the next stoplight—she is redefining the entire concept of "wear and tear."

When it comes to parking, she's learned to locate her position by sensing vibrations as the car brushes up against other objects. I am the only person I know with an automobile painted "rumpled brown."

While my daughter is performing all of these heart-stopping maneuvers, she is busy checking her makeup in the rearview mirror, tearing open candy wrappers, and chattering manically with her catatonic father. Her generation has evidently decided to abandon "defensive driving" in favor of "oblivious operation."

I'm not sure she learned anything more at Big Al's than she would have from an afternoon of bumper cars—but at least I got a coupon good for some free teeth-bleaching.

The Internals of the Combustion Engine

Apparently today's classrooms don't teach the inner workings of the automobile's engine anymore, figuring that it's good enough just to inform students that the exhaust pipe is the mechanism responsible for global warming. Thus it falls to the father to inject some science into the process of learning to drive, though the teenager rarely wants to cooperate, preferring to believe that the solution to car repair is simply to purchase a new automobile.

"I would never have a flat," my daughter sniffed when I suggested I teach her how to change one.

"But it could happen. You could run over a nail," I explained.

"Or an alligator with its mouth open," my son agreed. I frowned at him.

"Then I would call road service," she huffed.

"What if we don't have road service?"

"We don't have *road service*?" she demanded.

"Look, let's say it is a dark, rainy night. You are driving alone in the country, miles from any house, and you have a flat tire."

"I'd use the cell phone."

"Suppose you don't have the cell phone."

"It's ridiculous to drive without a cell phone."

"Okay. Okay. Suppose you are so far out in the country, your cell phone is out of range."

"And there's a guy with an axe chasing you," my son supplied helpfully.

I shook my head at him. "No axe murderers, just a flat tire."

"Well, I'm certainly not getting out in the rain," she sneered.

"Right." I inhaled carefully. "Okay, it stops raining. Now what are you going to do?"

"This is stupid. Why would I be out there in the first place?"

"I don't know. Your mother asked you to go to a farm and buy some fresh eggs. You got lost."

"Why wouldn't we just buy the eggs from the grocery store?"

"These are very *special* eggs," I suggested.

"They weigh five pounds each," my son interjected.

"Five *pounds*?" my daughter responded incredulously.

I gave my son a look.

"Well, you said they were special," he said defensively.

"I'm sure Mom would ask me to get eggs at *night*," my daughter sniffed.

My wife poked her head into the room. "What are you talking about?"

"Dad says we need eggs," my daughter answered.

My wife frowned. "No we don't."

"They're *magic* eggs," my son explained.

"What?"

"Not magic," I corrected. "I said 'special.' I'm teaching your daughter how to change a tire."

"Well, what on earth do eggs have to do with changing a tire?"

"Forget the eggs!" I shouted, exasperated. "Let's just focus on the flat tire, can we please?"

"How do I even know the tire is flat?"

"Aha!" I cried. The children blinked in surprise. Finally, a relevant question!

"Well, if it is your front tire, your steering gets all mushy. If it is your back tire, you'll feel a thumping sound, or a steady vibration."

"I'd just keep driving."

"Well no, you don't want to do that. If you keep driving on a flat, the rim shreds the rubber."

"Well, that's just stupid."

"You need to pull over."

"In the dark? In the country? Do you want me to be killed? There could be an axe murderer!"

"Or a giant chicken!" my son squealed gleefully.

"There are no murderers."

"Well, I'd keep driving until I came to a store or something."

"That would ruin the tire."

"I don't care. The stupid tire shouldn't have gone flat in the first place. It's not my fault."

"What you would want to do is pull over to the side of the road and change the tire."

"Well, I'm not doing that."

"You'd have to."

"I just won't go where my cell phone won't reach."

"Sometimes cell phones fail. Their batteries go dead from excess talking."

"We *do* need more batteries for the cell phone," she agreed.

"Well, you don't have any."

"Then I'm not going out into the country to buy giant eggs without Brian."

"I . . . Who the heck is Brian?"

"He's a guy."

"I assume that, but what does he have to do with this?"

"He knows all about cars. He always wants me to go for a ride with him."

"But you know never to ride with strangers," I admonished.

"Dad, he's not a stranger, he's *Brian*."

"He could be an axe murderer," I pointed out.

"Well, at least he knows how to change a tire."

I thought about my scenario—my daughter way out in the middle of nowhere, on a country road. At night, in the rain.

With Brian.

"Never mind. You should just call road service on the cell phone," I sighed.

"Can I play now, Dad?" my son wanted to know.

Conclusion

Parents often convince themselves that having another driver in the family is a good thing, something with which I'm sure insurance salesmen agree. While you're writing checks for auto premiums and gasoline charges, you'll tell yourself that it is so much more convenient now that your daughter is available to run to the store for you (or out to the country to fetch some special farm-fresh eggs, which I still insist is an entirely sensible activity).

And for the first few months after your government confers upon your daughter the legal right to drive, you'll find her almost irritatingly willing to run errands. "Need me to pick up cleaning? Do we need milk?" she'll press, until you're forced to come up with something just to get her to leave you alone. "Go get some eggs from the farm," you'll say.[1]

Teenagers will deny you even have the authority to prevent them from driving. They'll refer to the automobile

---

1. I guess I should explain that my wife was inappropriately skeptical that I would send my daughter out into the land of giant chickens in the middle of the night to get some eggs. The ensuing debate—during which I not only had to lay down the law and say that when I want fresh eggs I want fresh eggs, but also had to explain to my son that no, he couldn't have a pet chicken—took so long that my daughter left the room and had to be retrieved for the rest of my highly instructional lesson. When I reconstructed the dialogue for this book, I deliberately cut out my wife's rantings so readers wouldn't see how wrong she was about the eggs.

that you have purchased, maintained, and insured as "the" car. Not *your* car: *the* car, as not yours as the sky, the air. They also seem to believe that whatever social engagement they've arranged trumps any control you have over where your automobile is going: "I *have* to take the car, I'm going to a party!"

My advice is to sit them down and explain that their feet are still in working order and might reasonably be employed as an alternative method of transportation. Point out how much harder it was when you were a teenager and needed to walk nearly everywhere—they always appreciate hearing about that. If necessary, seize all the car keys and hold them hostage. That's your right: you're the father.

There Are Eight Simple Rules for Dating My Daughter

Unfortunately, No One
Seems to Be Paying Attention

Generally speaking, fathers are advised to take the following reasonable position when it comes to the subject of their daughters' dating: No.[1]

This is not (as we are often accused) because we don't want our daughters to have any fun in life. Indeed, I would be more than willing to spend hours and hours with my children, relating instructive and inspiring stories about my own childhood. Talk about fun!

We could also experience joy with the game I Got It! (a teen favorite), in which the teenage daughter reacts to the ringing of the phone by screaming, "I got it!" and knocks over chairs, TVs, and grandmothers to answer it first.

What I *don't* want my girls to play is any variation of the game Let's Grope. I find no value in having some teenage boy practice his hand-eye coordination on one of my daughters. You see, I remember my teenage years, a time of life when it is said a male's sexual function is at its peak. (Though how I could "peak" at something I wasn't even

[1]. A more lenient edict is, "Not until I'm dead and have been buried for at least three days."

doing is a concept I will never understand.) This is how we fathers know there is no such thing as a "nice" teenage boy.

> **Wife:** He won the National Science Award, he wants to be a pediatrician, and last week he pulled that family from that burning train. He's such a nice boy. Don't you think it would be okay if we had him over for supper?
>
> **Me:** Has he been castrated?
>
> **Wife:** Of course not!
>
> **Me:** Then no.

In fact, "burning train" is exactly what it feels like to be a teenage boy. Why would I want something like that in my own home?

Of course, the contemplation of this question implies that I have a choice in the matter. In my family, I have a vote in such concerns only if I am in agreement with my wife, who believes it is perfectly okay for complete strangers to arrive at my front door and remove one of my daughters from my protection for hours at a time, even though neither of them is wearing a radio collar or any other reasonable tracking aid.

"Don't you remember being that age?" she asks me patronizingly.

Of course I do. That's the point. But when I was in high school I used to be *terrified* of my girlfriend's father. He would open the door and immediately affect a good-naturedly murderous expression, holding out a handshake that, when gripped, felt like it could squeeze carbon into diamonds. Now, years later, recalling how unfairly persecuted I felt when I would pick up my dates, I do my best to make my daughters' suitors feel, well, even worse. My motto: wilt them in the living room and they'll stay wilted all night.

"I'm so glad to see you," I'll say sincerely. "I was afraid no boy would want to go out with my daughter after what I did to the last one."

As a dad, I have some basic rules, which I have carved into two stone tablets that are on display in my living room.

The Eight Simple Rules for Dating My Daughter

Rule Number One

If you pull into my driveway and honk, you'd better be delivering a package, because you're sure as heck not picking anything up.

Rule Number Two

Do not touch my daughter in front of me. You may glance at

her, so long as you do not peer at anything below her neck. If you cannot keep your eyes or hands off my daughter's body, I will remove them.

Rule Number Three

I am aware that it is considered fashionable for boys of your age to wear their trousers so loosely that they appear to be falling off their hips. This is utterly ridiculous—if you want to be stylish, you should look to me for cues. I've been dressing the same way for twenty years, and I still look great!

Nonetheless, I want to be fair and open-minded about this issue, so I propose this compromise: You may come to the door with your underwear showing and your pants ten sizes too big, and I will not object. However, in order to assure that your clothes do not, in fact, come off during the course of your date with my daughter, I will take my electric staple gun and fasten your trousers securely in place around your waist.

Rule Number Four

I'm sure you've been told that in today's world, sex without utilizing a "barrier method" of some kind can kill you.

Let me elaborate: when it comes to sex, I am the barrier, and I *will* kill you.

Rule Number Five

You may feel that in order for us to get to know each other, we should talk about sports, politics, and other issues of the day. Please do not do this. The only information I require from you is an indication of when you expect to have my daughter safely back at my house, and the only word I need from you on this subject is "early."

Rule Number Six

I have no doubt you are a popular fellow, with many opportunities to date other girls. This is fine with me as long as it is okay with my daughter. Otherwise, once you have gone out with my little girl, you will continue to date no one but her until she is finished with you. If you make her cry, I will make *you* cry.

Rule Number Seven

As you stand in my front hallway, waiting for my daughter to appear, and more than an hour goes by, please do not sigh and fidget. If you want to be on time for the movie, you should not be dating. Instead of just standing there, why don't you do something useful, like changing the oil in my car?

Rule Number Eight

The following places are not appropriate for a date with my daughter: places where there are beds, sofas, or anything softer than a wooden stool; places lacking parents, policemen, or nuns; places where there is darkness; places where there is dancing, holding hands, or happiness; places where the ambient temperature is warm enough to induce my daughter to wear shorts, tank tops, midriff T-shirts, or anything other than overalls, a sweater, and a goose-down parka zipped up to her chin. Movies with a strong romantic or sexual theme are to be avoided; movies that feature chain saws are okay. Hockey games are okay.

My daughters claim it embarrasses them to come downstairs and find me attempting to get their dates to recite these eight simple rules from memory. I'd be embarrassed too—there are only eight of them, for crying out loud! And for the record, I did *not* suggest to one of these nice boys that I'd have these rules tattooed on his arm if he couldn't remember them. (I checked into it and the cost is prohibitive.) I merely told him that I thought writing the rules on his arm with a ballpoint might be inadequate—ink washes off. (I brought up my wood-burning set as a joke. I don't know why everyone made such a big deal about it.)

A Reasonable Father's Thoughts on Curfew

The concept of curfew is simple enough: it is the designated time by which the nice boy dating your daughter must have her back in your house or be subject to arrest. I'm actually very open-minded when it comes to curfew: as long as the sun is still up, I'm willing to accept a fairly late curfew. (This rule naturally changes during daylight saving time.)

Teenagers don't comprehend the purpose of curfew, which has got nothing to do with making sure they are home at a decent hour (or as they insist, to punish them for "being alive"). The sole purpose of curfew is to allow you, the father, to sleep at night. Yet no matter how carefully you overreact when your daughters stay out late, they just don't seem to understand. It's almost as if teens think about something other than Dad's Rules when out on a date!

Now, be advised that the one person your daughter should *not* ask about curfew is her mother. Who knows what crazy answer a woman will give a daughter who asks what time she should be home? Even worse, mothers often do not take the time to explain to the nice boy what will happen to him if he brings his date home even one minute after curfew, whereas a father will painstakingly walk the boy through the consequences, using chopping and strangling gestures with his hands, in order that the young man retains a graphic picture in his mind. This can be very helpful to the nice boy.

Despite this show-and-tell, all daughters will experiment at least once with violating curfew. This is the "error" in the "trial and error" method. Having been through the experience of waiting for a daughter to get home from her date myself, I can offer advice to fathers as to the do's and don'ts of curfew violation.

Do's and Don'ts for Fathers During Curfew Violation

DON'T   Sleep. Let's face it, it would be easier to sleep if you were being licked in the face by your dog than to try to doze off while your daughter is out past curfew. If you lie in bed, you will wind up twisting the sheets into a tight cocoon, which will cut off all circulation in your legs and hamper your wife's breathing. Worse, thrashing around in the dark allows your mind to wander into areas where, believe me, you don't want to go. It will suddenly occur to you that your daughter's date bears an uncommon resemblance to Ted Kennedy. A review of the simple rules for dating your daughter reveals what you've long suspected: eight is *not* enough. You'll recall being sixteen and how much room you had to maneuver in the backseat of your dad's Buick—and when you remember just which maneuvers you were attempting, you'll flash into an awakened state for which "insomnia" is a totally inadequate description.

DO Call the boy's father. Hey, you're not sleeping; he shouldn't be sleeping either. If he sounds a little smug about the fact that his kid is the burning train in this scenario, dampen his mood by telling him your daughter is coming down with the Ebola virus or, even worse, is planning to run for Congress—you want him to be focused on separating his son from your daughter in every sense of the word. (If you employ this tactic, you run the risk of the father denying his son permission to date your daughter ever again. I must warn you, however, that you can't always count on this outcome.)

DON'T Contact the National Dairy Association to see about putting your daughter's face on milk cartons. I've called those people and they are completely unhelpful, especially after they begin to recognize your voice. They've got some stupid rule about an hour being too soon to go public.

If you sarcastically point out that if Paul Revere had waited for an hour before getting on his horse to warn the army at Pearl Harbor that the British were coming, we'd all be speaking British today, they'll pretend they have no idea what you're talking about.

DO Call the police. They have guns, pepper spray, and clubs, all of which are of great comfort as you picture them conducting a manhunt for your daughter's date. They're just as eager to deploy helicopters and bloodhounds as you are—that's why most of them became cops: for the toys. Be aware, however, that they get rather testy if you claim that your child was forcibly taken from your home and then it turns out you aren't able to provide them with evidence of a struggle. Focus on the facts: a predator is holding your daughter against your will. And don't let the police question your wife, who is likely to come up with a completely false version of events.

DON'T Telephone the places they said they would be going. You'll find movie theaters completely unwilling to stop the show and turn up the house lights to search for your daughter. Restaurants will refuse to evacuate and hold all their customers in the parking lot until you get there, and when you phone a rock concert they can't even *hear* you. This lack of cooperation will only increase your anxiety level to about the same as the shower scene in *Psycho*.

DO Get in your car and drive around to look for them. You'll feel better if you do *something*. Even more rewarding is the look on your daughter's friends' faces when you pull up to them and frantically ask if they've seen her. The next day they will call your daughter and tell her about the incident, and your child will be absolutely mortified. This punishment will seem even worse than the fact that you've grounded her until she's fifty-four years old.

DON'T Wake up your wife. She will accuse you of being ridiculous, which will just prove to you that she has no idea what is going on. So what if they're "only" five minutes late? Five minutes is *plenty* of time—doesn't she remember your honeymoon?

DO Practice what you are going to say to the nice boy upon their return. Don't worry about sounding like a madman: you're a man, and you're mad—how are you supposed to sound?

The Prom

If your daughter's dates are like piranhas, eating away at your sanity a bite at a time, prom is like a great white shark, totally consuming your mental well-being in a single gulp. For reasons that must be hardwired into the X chromosomes, women feel that prom is the one night of the year when all rules relating to curfew, conduct, and common sense are suspended. It's no longer a question of what time your daughter will be coming home, but what *day*.

Boys have every intention of taking advantage of this relaxation of parental intelligence. When I was a high school senior, all the boys in my class figured that asking a girl to prom was pretty darn close to taking one on a honeymoon, except that no one threw a bouquet and you didn't have to dance with your mother.

Adding fuel to this fire is the prom dress, an outfit you would never give permission for your daughter to wear but that you are supposed to pay for anyway.

The Prom Dress

A prom dress costs anywhere from 75 to 200 percent more than you can afford to pay. When I was in high school, prom dresses consisted primarily of two elements: "poof" and "fluff." I remember peering at my date's dress and wondering if her body was still there among all the hostile puffery and how I might access it through what appeared to be a hundred yards of extraneous cloth. (My efforts were, as it turned out, a waste of mental activity. She disappeared into the ladies' room shortly after we arrived and emerged only occasionally to see if I was still there.)

Today, prom dresses consist of "slits" and "skin." Their primary function seems to be to set the train on fire, if you get my drift. Should you take heart medication, be sure to have it close at hand the first time your daughter models her prom dress for you. Your wife will proclaim the dress "cute," which shows that women should not be allowed to use the English language. Puppies are cute. Your daughter in her prom dress is nothing at all like a puppy. When you are finally able to speak, you are likely to have a conversation like this with your wife.

You: Where's the rest of it?

Wife: You mean the ribbon for her hair? We haven't been able to find one expensive enough yet.

You: I mean the clothing for her body! I distinctly remember getting a Visa bill for a dress. This isn't a dress, it's an advertisement for sex.

Wife: Oh shush, it's cute.

You: Cute? Are you listening to yourself? I suppose her date will be dressed as a pimp!

Wife: It's a darling dress.

You: Isn't it dangerous to show so much cleavage? I thought cleavage could only be let out a little at a time. Won't she catch pneumonia?

Wife: Doesn't it look good with her eyes?

You: What, her breasts? Her breasts look good with her eyes?

Wife: I'm so glad we could find those shoes.

The Prom Date

This year, my younger daughter isn't going to prom, owing primarily to the fact that I put my foot down and denied her permission to go, and not because she didn't get asked by anybody, despite what my wife thinks.

My older daughter is, of course, going—if no one had asked *her*, I assume she would have driven to the nearest wedding, found a male in a tux, and dragged him to prom (even if he were the groom). Alas, she had plenty of invitations, which meant we were all subjected to a nightly monologue entitled "With Whom Shall I Go to Prom, Let Me Reflect on My List of Choices Because I Am So Popular." My son and I perfected our gagging noises so we could provide suitable background music to this litany.

She assures me I will really like the boy she has chosen because he has a great sense of humor. As evidence, she announces the fact that he has dyed his hair electric blue "just to be weird." I reply it sounds like he accomplished his goal. Ha ha, see, you have a sense of humor too, my daughter teases.

Now, I've met Mr. Blue Hair. He looks like the victim of a jewelry store explosion: his face is full of shrapnel— rings and studs all over the place. He likes to reach out and put a protective arm around my daughter, although as far as I am concerned it is *he* who needs protection. My wife wants to know if we should set out hors d'oeuvres for the two of them. Why? I ask. It's not enough I'm giving him my daughter, I have to *feed him* too? Ha ha, my daughter laughs. Dad, you have such a sense of humor. Ho ho, I chortle. Here are the Special Additional Rules for your prom:

1. No area of his epidermis may touch any area of your epidermis.

2. I am going with you.

Naturally, my wife advises my daughter "not to listen" to her father—as if anyone ever listens anyway. Why does she need to go to prom? I demand. She's only in high school!

On prom night Mr. Blue Hair shows up right on time, wearing a muted gray tux—from the neck down he appears perfectly normal; from the neck up he looks like he's just wandered in from the set of *The X-Files*. Observing the leer on his face as he watches his date come down the stairs, I presume that the theme of this year's party is "I Am Planning to Take Advantage of Your Daughter."

When I follow his gaze, I find myself momentarily unable to speak. Her long hair carefully curled, her face subtly made up, my daughter is suddenly a young woman so lovely, it occurs to me that she simply isn't my little girl anymore. She's all grown up.

Well, I snap out of *that* in a hurry.

After some nervous tittering by everybody, my wife sets out to make this the most documented event in history, employing at least three separate cameras and urging us all into a series of absurd poses. "Okay, honey. You, your dad, and the dog holding a rose in its teeth, over there by the fireplace," she commands.

"David," I say to my daughter's date between photographs, "may I have a word with you?"

"It's Derek, Bruce," he responds jovially. As he reluctantly removes his hand from my daughter's bare shoulder I realize I've developed a facial tic.

"It's Mr. Cameron, Derek," I agree kindly. I try not to dwell on his name—a derrick is one of those things that stick out from the side of a ship. The mental image makes me nauseated. What kind of parents name their kid after something like that? I usher Mr. Ship Sticker out of earshot of the two women.

Assuming a warm, fatherly expression, my arm across his shoulder, I get directly to the matter on my mind. "Derek, do you know what an autopsy is?"

He blinks. "Uh, I think."

"What is an autopsy, Derek?" I encourage.

"Is it where they determine the cause of death?" he responds, looking a little worried at the direction the conversation is taking.

"Right! Now, Derek, let me ask you this: do you want to have an autopsy?"

"No?" he guesses.

"Of course not," I agree. "Because if you lay a hand on my daughter, we already *know* what your cause of death will be, don't we?"

He glances miserably back at his date, who isn't paying attention. His finger nervously strokes the ring in his eyebrow, and I must physically restrain myself from yanking it like a rip cord.

"So what are we *not going to do*, Derek?" I prod.

"Lay your daughter," he mumbles.

"Lay a hand on my daughter," I correct sternly.

"Oh. Yeah."

I can see by his unhappiness that he's gotten the message. I clap him on the shoulder and am gratified at the way he flinches. "You kids go on and have fun, now."

He scurries back to his date, and for the first time that night, I smile.

Group Dating

A relatively new concept in male-female relations is the idea that an entire group of young people will go out on a single date. No particular person is paired with another— they just swarm together like a bunch of insects in heat. How the heck is a father supposed to know whom to intimidate under these conditions? Worse, these group dates often wind up at someone's house, where the entire lot of them *spend the night* sleeping on the floor!

"Oh, Dad," your daughter will say, "nothing's going to happen with all those people there!"

This just goes to show the sad state of education in America today, because if your daughter knew anything about history, she'd know that the most horrible things that have ever taken place were because there were all those people there! When was the last time a war or a plague happened to just one person? Can a single individual have an orgy or a riot?

"I've met the parents," your wife will say. "They're nice."

Great! That's just who you want watching over your child as she lies sprawled among a bunch of teenage boys: a couple of "nice" parents. Wouldn't you feel more comfortable if your wife said, "I've met the parents. She's a professional wrestler and he's a prison guard."

You are perfectly within your rights as a father to come up with some Special Additional Rules for Group Dates, such as

1. Only at my house.

2. I will sit in the center of the sprawl with a bottle of No-Doz in one hand and a cattle prod in another. If I see any boy attempting to get into the wrong sleeping bag, I will prod him back into the proper place.

Conclusion

Sadly, there is no real way to prevent your daughter from dating. However, with judicious application of your physical presence into most of her social situations, you may be able to prevent her from enjoying it very much. It is always possible to purchase a seat in a movie ("Hey, kids, I'm sitting right behind you if you want some of my popcorn!") or find a table in a restaurant ("Wow, what a coincidence, third time this week!") near where your daughter and the nice young man with the blue hair are trying to be alone with each other.

Just remember: you don't want them doing what you did, or trying to do what you tried to do, or thinking about what you thought about. That's your prerogative: you're the father.

The First Job

A Failure in the Welfare-to-Work Program

A body at rest tends to remain at rest,[1] giving you the feeling that your teenage daughter will probably continue to live in your house until she goes on Social Security. She'll ignore subtle hints, like "You are the laziest person on earth" and "When I was your age I had *two* jobs," waving at you irritably because you are interfering with her phone call.

"I don't have *time* to get a job," she'll explain. Apparently between not doing her chores, not picking up her room, and not doing her homework, her schedule is exhausting enough already.

Then everything changes: one of her friends gets a job at the mall, and within a week your jaw drops in amazement as your daughter unfolds the want ads and begins marking them up with a pen.

"Dad, what's a COO?" she asks.

"Chief operating officer."

"Would I like that?" she wonders, her pen ready to circle the ad. She squints at you over the top of the newspaper.

1. Sir Isaac Newton, describing his teenage daughter.

"I think you have to have a college degree for that one," you tell her.

"Oh, right," she mutters. "Well, it sounds like a stupid job anyway."

"Try to find one that doesn't ask for qualifications," her younger sister advises.

"Here's one," she says. "Corporate buyer. Well, I know I could do *that* job." Her eyes sparkle.

"Maybe you should shoot for something a little lower on the totem pole just to start out with," you suggest.

"Yeah, like the part of the totem pole that sticks under the ground," her sister observes.

Eventually she decides the local restaurants represent the best place to start her career. "I'd work in a clothing shop at the mall," she explains, "but then everyone would think all my clothes came from that one store because of my employee discount."

Take my advice: you really don't want to understand this comment.

Preparing for the Job Interview

"Let's say I'm the employer, and you're coming in to interview for the job," I tell my daughter.

"I don't want to do that," she responds.

"Don't you think you need some practice with the job interview process? You've never done it before."

"How would *you* know anything about it?" she demands. "Did you ever own a restaurant?"

"No, but I've applied for work a number of times before."

She rolls her eyes. "Whatever."

"Okay, here. You come in through the door there and I'll interview."

She stands up as if weighted down with cement. "Okay, fine." She walks out the door, turns around, and saunters back in. "Satisfied?"

"Hello, Ms. Cameron, it's good to meet you," I greet her warmly, holding out my hand. She gives me a dead-fish handshake, slouching into her chair.

"You should wait until I invite you to sit down," I tell her.

"Oh, I'm sure they're going to say *that*."

"No, I'm giving you advice now as your father. When you go in for your interview, wait to be asked before you sit down. And when you sit, don't collapse. Sit up straight."

She waves a hand dismissively.

"Now, Ms. Cameron, tell me, have you ever had experience busing tables before?"

"This is stupid."

"Sorry?"

"It says right on my application that I haven't."

"Right. But the person you're talking to might not remember that. He's been interviewing a lot of people for this job, you know, and his questions have started to fall into a pattern."

"Well, if he's not even going to read the application, why did I bother to fill it out?"

I think about that one. "I don't know, you'll have to ask them."

She snaps her bubble gum, nodding.

"Now, do you have any experience busing tables?"

"Well, my dad makes me do the dishes all the time at home, even though all he does is sit on his butt and watch stupid sports on television."

I frown. "What stupid sports?"

"Like those boats with the giant fans on the back that go racing around in the swamp."

"Well, I'm sure your father is tired from all his hard work earning a living and deserves to take a break."

"He just sits there and belches."

I take a deep breath. "All right, Ms. Cameron. The person we're looking for must be neat and orderly. Would you say you keep your room picked up?"

"That's the stupidest question I've ever heard. I'm sure they're going to ask that."

"But what if they do?"

"I would refuse to answer."

"You *can't* refuse to answer, it's a job interview!"

"It's against the Constitution!"

"No it's not. They can ask whatever they want as long as they aren't discriminatory."

"Well, I think *this* is discriminatory."

"They are just trying to get a feel for the type of person you are. Are you neat, orderly, and organized, or are you a complete slob who never puts her clothes away?"

"This is so hypocritical."

"What? How is it hypocritical?"

"Okay, just forget it. Yes, my room is picked up."

"That would be a lie, now, wouldn't it?"

"Oh, you mean the restaurant sends people out to photograph my room to see if I'm lying about it? Does that mean they'll take pictures of you drinking beer?"

"I'm speaking as your father."

"Forget it. I'm not even going to *go* if they're going to ask all these questions."

"They have to ask questions, it is an interview. That's what an interview *is*, they ask questions."

"Well, that doesn't mean I have to answer them."

"Do you want the job, or not?"

"No if you're my father, and yes if it's the interview."

"I'm not sure I understand."

"Are we done?"

"No. Now, normally they'll ask if *you* have any questions."

"No."

"No what?"

"No, I don't have any questions."

"You really should ask questions, it shows them you are interested."

"Dad, it's *busing tables*. What am I going to ask—'What color is the rubber tub?'"

"No, now give it some thought. What sort of question could you pose that will show you are bright, hardworking, and responsible?" I stare at her telepathically.

She frowns, then brightens. "I know! How about, 'Do you give bonuses at Christmas?'"

"Well . . . I was thinking more along the lines of asking if there was any opportunity for advancement."

"If I ask that they'll think my father told me to."

"Why do you say that?"

"Because only a father would think to ask if you could get *promoted* from a job wiping off tables," she snorts scornfully.

And she's right . . . but wouldn't the world be a better place if everyone *did* think like a father?

The High Cost of Employment

For some reason, everyone in the family expects the father to cough up the money to underwrite the job search. These funds go into the general "I'll pay you back" pool, which I calculate to be at roughly $12,000. "Why do you need a new outfit to interview for a job as a buser?" I demand.

My wife frowns at me. "It's her first job interview, she needs confidence," she tells me.

"I'd like to have some confidence that I'll get repaid for this," I reply.

"Oh, don't worry, Dad, I'll pay you back," my daughter promises. "I'll have a job!"

Here are the expenses incurred by my daughter, and therefore by me, in her quest for a minimum-wage job:

ITEM	COST
Two new outfits for job interviews	$160
New shoes for new outfits	$ 90
Haircut for job interview	$ 40
New leather portfolio for taking notes in job interview	$ 40
New pen for taking notes in the new portfolio	$ 29
Gasoline—4 job interviews	$ 25

ITEM	COST
Parking ticket—first interview	$ 15
Parking ticket—second interview	$ 15
Parking ticket—third interview	$ 15
Parking ticket—fourth interview	$ 15
Speeding ticket	$ 55
Tab for celebration dinner—got the job!	$ 75
Uniform for work	$ 60
New shoes for work	$ 34
Parking pass for work	$ 50
Total	$718

I am officially on record as declaring this to be a lot of money, and make the suggestion that perhaps the first couple of paychecks could be used for repayment.

"You want me to give you money out of my *paycheck*?" my daughter demands. "Why am I even bothering to work, then?"

"I thought you said you were going to reimburse me for all of this stuff?"

"Yes, but not out of my *paycheck*. Out of money I have left over!"

In other words, I'll never see a dime of it. I've been working for a long time now, and I know from experience: there's never any money "left over."

Daughter on the Job

Preparing for the first day on the job was a crisis that involved the entire family, my daughter racing around barking orders like the captain of a burning ship.

"I can't find my earrings!" she shrieked.

"The ones with the little diamonds in them?" her sister asked.

"No, not those! I could never wear those to work! I have to wear little silver hoops."

"The silver hoops are mine," her sister pointed out.

"Would you please just go get them? I have to go to work! I don't have time to argue! I'm going to be late!"

"Why don't you let your sister borrow them just this once, until she can get her own pair?" my wife suggested.

New silver hoop earrings $67

"I can't find my shoes! Where's my hairbrush? No one is helping me!" she cried.

"Here are your shoes. Here's your hairbrush. How can I help you?" my wife answered gently.

"How old do you have to be before your mother stops dressing you?" I asked, earning me the Dirty Look Award for Sarcastic Observation Posed as a Question.

"Is there gas in the car? Did someone fill the tank?"

Gasoline for first day on the job $25

"Is my uniform straight? I look ugly in these pants! I hate my job, I hate it!"

"You look fine," my wife soothed.

"Dad, I need to borrow your car."

"What? What's wrong with your mother's car?"

"Oh, like I'm going to drive the *minivan* to work," she sneered.

"Well, what am I supposed to do if I need to go somewhere?" I asked reasonably.

"You'll just have to make do until we can find a car for her to drive," my wife told me.

Used car $4,500

Finally we managed to shove my daughter out the door. She laid down twin tracks of rubber in the driveway as she rocketed out into the street and blasted away.

"Let's go to the restaurant and see how she's doing," my wife suggested.

"Are you kidding? We just got rid of her. Let's enjoy the postcalamity silence," I responded.

"It'll be fun."

"Absolutely not!"

When we got to the restaurant, my daughter was nowhere in sight. "She's been fired already," I predicted.

"Hush," my wife responded. "Let's sit down and order."

We slid into a booth and a few moments later were rewarded with the vision of my daughter bursting out of the kitchen, lugging a plastic tub. I watched in amazement as she determinedly swept the dishes away from the countertop, vigorously wiping down its surface with a rag.

"What's she doing?" my son wanted to know, whispering. He'd never seen anything like it before, and lacked the vocabulary to describe what he was witnessing.

"Working," I replied in astonishment.

Like a bee pollinating a flower bed, she shot over to another table, scooping away the remains of a dinner with quick efficiency. The rag came back out. Done. On to the next.

"Call the police. They've given her amphetamines," I told my wife.

A couple were immediately seated at the table my daughter had just wiped. The man picked up a menu, then rubbed his arm. "Hey," he said loudly. "This table's still wet."

"That's because it's clean," I advised him from across the room.

My wife put a hand on my wrist.

"What?" he answered me, puzzled that a complete stranger should be so helpful.

"It's clean. They do a real good job of keeping their tables wiped down here. The staff is real attentive."

"I'm sorry, but who asked you?" he wanted to know. "I'm sitting down here and I'm getting my sleeves wet."

"Maybe if you didn't lean on the table when you read, that wouldn't happen," I said kindly. "Try not to move your lips, either."

"Bruce," my wife warned.

The guy looked over at his date. "Can you believe this guy?" he demanded.

A waitress popped into view. "Can I get you all something to drink?" she asked them brightly, pulling out a notepad.

"Listen, this tabletop is still wet," he told her.

"It's clean," I insisted, coming over to join the conversation. Out of the corner of my eye, I could see my wife gesturing, probably in complete support. "See, he just doesn't appreciate how spotless it is."

The waitress frowned at me as if unsure why I was involved in the discussion.

"You can see your reflection in it," I added helpfully.

"Look, can I speak to the manager?" the belligerent demanded.

"That might be a good idea," I agreed. "In fact, if you want to assemble all the employees, this might be an excellent opportunity to show them how to deal with morons who don't appreciate antiseptic eating conditions." I turned and gave my wife a thumbs-up sign. Her expression didn't communicate the appreciation I felt appropriate to the situation.

Later my wife complained rather bitterly about not being able to stay for dinner. "I can't believe you got us thrown out of a family restaurant," she fumed.

"We were not thrown out. We were simply asked to leave because that guy wouldn't stop arguing with me," I corrected.

"All he wanted was a dry table!"

"And eventually he got one, didn't he? It's called evaporation," I explained scientifically.

"Were you really going to punch him in the nose?" my son wanted to know.

"I've never been so embarrassed in my life," my wife stated.

"That's what you always say about our wedding," I pointed out. "You can't have it both ways."

"I'm just glad our daughter didn't see us, she would have been mortified."

"The guy was a jerk," I said defensively. "He's probably an escaped war criminal."

"He said he was a Presbyterian minister."

"Right, like a minister would be on a date with some bimbo!"

"That was his wife!"

Well, clearly I had won that argument, and there was no sense talking about it further.

When my daughter came home, I said nothing about the brief altercation at the restaurant, though when I mentioned that I was sorry she had to deal with "a bunch of rude customers" my wife shot me a warning look.

"I'm exhausted," my daughter declared, falling onto the couch. "I can't move. Will someone massage my feet?"

"Did you have fun?"

"Fun! I worked for nearly four hours straight!" Her shoes thumped to the floor. "My back aches. Can someone bring me something to drink?" She placed a hand over her eyes. "You have *no idea* what it's like to work that hard."

"Is that so?" I replied.

"Mom, you'll have to wash this uniform tonight, I got real sweaty. I ordered another one so you won't have to do this every time."

Second uniform $60

The next morning was Saturday, and my wife's list of things for me to accomplish included a number of items I felt more appropriate for the children to do. "You can cut the grass," I informed my older daughter.

"What? But I *work*."

"What time do you go to the restaurant?"

"Four o'clock."

"Well it's not even noon yet. You have plenty of time."

"But I have to work all weekend! Have someone else do it, I'm too tired!"

"Just because you have a job doesn't mean you no longer have to participate in the weekend chores," I told her.

"That's not fair! I work until closing tonight!" She got up, throwing down her napkin. "Nobody else in this family works as hard as I do!"

"Hey, would you mind wiping down the table?" I called after her. Only my son thought it was funny.

Conclusion

On the issue of employment, your expert advice is critical and will be completely ignored. You'll point out that your daughter has taken a job with no plan for how she's going to get there—apparently, *you're* in charge of transportation services, and you'd better make sure you don't schedule a conflict between your own professional responsibilities and your child's minimum-wage job. "I'd really like to stay late and finish this project," you'll find yourself telling your boss, "but my daughter needs to get to work."

When the first paychecks roll in, your lecture series on

Saving for College will be unattended, though you will be asked to teach a class on Why Do I Have to Pay Social Security? I Don't Even *Like* Old People. Be prepared for your daughter to expend considerable outrage—a lot of Republicans are born at moments like these.

The first job's impact on family finances is negligible—though your daughter now presumably has more money, it doesn't mean she'll ask you for less. The only real change you'll notice is on her schedule: where it used to drive you crazy that she'd constantly be underfoot on the weekends, yakking on the phone or watching TV, now she's not home at all, and it puts odd holes in your day. When she walks in the door you'll quiz her about work, as if scooping dishes into a rubber tub is a fascinating activity. You miss her, though you won't express any misgivings about this spark of ambition. You have to encourage this, to give the little bird a gentle kick in the tail feathers as she stands poised on the edge of the nest. This is your role: you're the father.

The
Boyfriend

Without Even Consulting the Father, a Boy Is Granted Special Access to the Teenage Daughter

One day it will suddenly occur to you that the pack of boys sniffing around one of your daughters has dramatically thinned, leaving a single alpha male who will begin hanging out at your house like a son adopted without any paperwork, eating dinner with you and attempting to engage you in unwelcome conversation: a boyfriend.

The English language has been so thoroughly corrupted by teenagers, you can't even get a straight answer about the intended role of this loiterer. "We're going out," your older daughter will explain, though what actually happens is they spend more time staying *in*, as far as you can tell.

"You mean you're going steady?" you'll demand.

Hysterical laughter is the response, leaving you no closer to the truth.

"Oh Dad, no one goes *steady* anymore."

You ponder this. On the face of it, this sounds like a positive development, one you can support—except that you have a feeling you are not going to like the alternative.

"Didn't you 'go out with' Derek?" you demand.

"We went on a couple of dates, but we didn't go *out*," she replies scornfully.

"So, when you go out with this new boy, you aren't going out on a *date*?"

"Oh, Dad."

Is it so unreasonable to ask that we agree on common terms so I'll understand what I'm trying to prohibit?

Don't Look To Your Wife for Help

Women don't seem to understand that there is a big difference between having wolves out there in the woods and letting one move inside and sit in your favorite chair. Point this out to them, though, and they'll look at you like you're crazy. "He's such a nice boy!" your wife will say.

That again.

I tend to sort teenage boys into two categories: "unwelcome" and "rejected." And while it is true that I'd have to agree with my wife that this unauthorized boy who has started showing up every day seems relatively harmless, how can I be sure?

"His father was chaperon at the same school party where you danced with that woman all night," my wife notes, stuffing so many irrelevancies into a single sentence I can't count them all. I've already explained that she wasn't a woman, she was a teacher. Second, though I cannot obtain confirmation from either of my daughters, I suspect it was at this very same high school dance that this whole problem started—that it was this same boy who dragged my unsuspecting child into the gym and clung to her. If the presence of two fathers isn't enough to quell this boy's predatory instincts, clearly the situation is far worse than anyone could imagine.

"What have you got against him?" my wife asks repeatedly. Obviously, she is not paying any attention to my answer, so I will spell it out here.

Here's What I Have Against Him, Along with My Wife's Irrelevant Responses

Me: His name is Blunt. What kind of name is that?

My Wife: *His name is not Blunt. It's Blaine. It was his grandfather's name.*

Me: Why do his lips have to be so close to my daughter's lips? It's like they've become Siamese twins, joined at the face.

My Wife: *They're in love, dear. Can't you see how happy your daughter is?*

Me: I do not recall giving permission for anybody to fall in love.

My Wife: *He helps me carry in the groceries, which*

none of her other boyfriends have ever volunteered to do.

Me: That's because the faster we get the food in the house, the faster he can eat it! Do you have to feed him all the time? If you feed him, he will just become dependent on us, and won't be able to fend for himself in the wild.

My Wife: *Boys his age have such a strong appetite.*

Me: It is his "appetites" that I'm worried about! Do the two of them have to hold on to each other all the time? It's not natural.

My Wife: *Honey, there's nothing in the world more natural.*

Me: He's here every day. His parents must not care where he is or what he does. He was probably raised by wolves.

My Wife: *His parents are wonderful people. In fact, I've invited them over for dinner next weekend.*

Me: Oh great, now we have to feed the *parents*, too? Why can't our daughter just become pen pals with Blunt, give the relationship time? If, after ten or fifteen years, the two of them find they are still attracted to each other, and I approve of his employment, *then* they can start "going out." This is a very reasonable proposal and I need your support here.

My Wife: *Would you please stop calling him that, you embarrass all of us.*

Me: Our daughter is too young to get so serious about a boy! She has her whole life ahead of her, and I don't want to spend it with this boy!

My Wife: *What have you got against him?*

Truthfully, I'm not sure. He *does* seem like a "nice boy," which immediately makes me suspicious. For example, the first time I met him and gave him the Eight Simple Rules, subjecting him to a Standard Paternal Interrogation, he answered all of my questions clearly, looking me in the eye as he did so. Most of the boys who come over usually start fidgeting when I demand to know the terms of their probation. Blunt just laughed and told me he'd never even had a traffic ticket. Wonderful. As any police officer will tell you, there is no more dangerous felon than the one they can never seem to catch.

One way your daughter's new boyfriend differs from the other males in the pack is that she and he share a "relationship." This may strike you as entirely inappropriate—your daughter is too young to have such a thing.

Relationships convert magnetism into electricity, which is then, more often than not, used to shock the father. You'll come around the corner, and in a sensation that feels akin to what pilots call "sudden decompression," you'll find your daughter and Blunt folded into an easy chair in the living room, just sitting together as if they are doing their part to combat a national chair shortage. Unfortunately, no little orange masks drop from the ceiling to help you pull in oxygen—you're forced to gasp on your own.

"Blunt," you say when you find your voice, "I think that big pine tree in the backyard is getting root rot, would you mind taking a look?"

"No problem!" he agrees genially, springing to his feet and sprinting out the door. Your daughter squints at you. "Root rot?" she demands.

"That chair is not structurally sound," you tell her. "I suggest you sit on a stool. Or just stand."

This relationship factor has caused my wife's sensibilities to completely collapse, to the point where she has been giving my daughter permission to violate some of my absolute, carved in stone, I-really-mean-it paternal proclamations.

"Where is she?" I fume. "I told her to be home at midnight, and it is nearly two minutes after."

"I said they could stay out until one o'clock," my wife responds smoothly.

My eyes bulge. "One o'clock, are you crazy? Do you think that just because we've fed him five hundred dollars' worth of groceries the past month, he'll leave our daughter alone? Look, when a boy becomes a steady date, you make the curfew even earlier, not later."

"What on earth are you talking about?"

My exasperation could not be more complete. "Okay, I guess I have to explain this to you in language you'll understand." (This earns me a dark look, but I plunge on.) "See, the first couple of times a boy is up to bat, he'll probably strike out. At best, he fouls a couple into the stands. He might get to first base, but that's it. But you give him enough at bats, and he becomes accustomed to the curves of the pitches."

"*This* is language I'm supposed to understand?"

I will not be deterred. "Before long, getting to third base happens on the first swing. He becomes a home run hitter. Do you realize what I am talking about here? You've let your daughter stay out until one o'clock in the morning with Babe Ruth!"

"What I realize is that you're comparing your daughter to a baseball diamond. How nice. Next you'll be saying she's a hill and Blaine's the enemy army."

This is one of the serious disadvantages of being married for so long: your wife begins to anticipate your arguments. "Well, I wasn't going to say she was a *hill*, exactly," I sputter.

My wife isn't the only person who has suspended all the rules that would normally apply in our household. My daughter has gotten into the act, dropping the competitive edge and pretending a helplessness that I find baffling. "Blaine, would you come over and help me wash the car?" she beseeches into the phone.

Now, to the casual observer, this seems a pretty innocuous request, but I know my daughter. Washing the car in the driveway isn't something she would ever actually *do*, not when for a mere $10 of her father's money she can drive into a machine that sprays foam on your automobile for thirty seconds and then rinses it off. Now that she has Blunt in her life, however, the car becomes a prop, an excuse for her to put on a bathing suit and a T-shirt and run around squealing, allowing herself to be sprayed with the hose. My daughter *squealing*? I would have told you confidently that if anybody came over and sprayed her with the hose, she would grab it and stuff the nozzle down his throat. But all that has changed with the arrival of Blunt.

"You're getting all wet, honey," I tenderly tell my daughter as I drape a rubber raincoat over her shoulders. I carefully zip it up, admiring the way it repels water and lust. She balks when I attempt to coax her to step into a pair of fishing waders, however, even though the raincoat has left her ankles scandalously exposed.

Another rule that has apparently been rendered void is the one that states that to be on time for curfew, one must be in the house and thoroughly debriefed by the appointed hour. With Blunt in our lives, it now seems to be okay with everybody else if his car is merely *in the driveway* by curfew—and then it just sits there, giving me hot and cold flashes and causing me to pace around repeating, "What are they *doing*?" to myself even though, to be truthful, I don't actually want to know. After fiddling with the lights, flashing them off and on a few times and beaming a powerful flashlight at the car in such a manner that any other two people on earth would get the hint, I'm forced to go outside and pretend to inspect the rain gutters, bumping into the car with the ladder a few times until the doors open.

"Dad, why are you doing that right now?" my daughter demands peevishly.

"Well, hello!" I call gaily. "What a surprise. I didn't realize you were out here. I assumed that since it is past curfew you were already safe inside the house."

"Would you like some help with that, Mr. Cameron?" Blunt asks. Oh, he thinks he has me fooled, but I'm not falling for it.

"Actually, yes, if you wouldn't mind moving your car back to your house, that would make this easier," I tell him.

What would really make this easier is if he'd move his car back to his house and leave it there, but you don't mention this. Despite the fact that this interloper is a brand-new addition to your family, his popularity polls are higher than yours. For the time being, you're just going to have to tolerate his pestiferous presence.

The Goodnight Kiss Incident

As any reasonable father knows, teenage girls should not be kissing teenage boys. To prevent this from happening, fathers are urged to do everything possible to reduce romantic influences. Normally, standing around in my bathrobe and checking the rain gutters is highly effective in this regard. With a steady boyfriend, however, even my best chaperon frown cannot seem to forestall an inappropriate commingling of oral bacteria. Even though I am lingering there, clearing my throat, coughing lightly, and murmuring, "That's enough, now," they still engage in a goodnight kiss whose purpose seems to be to subject their brains to oxygen deprivation.

As with a dogfight, you must resist the almost overwhelming impulse to thrust your hand between the two and attempt to separate them. A better solution is to use the garden hose, but don't expect any support from the rest of your family if you do so.

"Hey, but it was okay when they were washing the car!" you'll protest in an argument for the defense so compelling any judge in the world would enter a directed verdict of Not Guilty—This Man Is a Hero. Unfortunately, your wife isn't willing to hear evidence at the trial, and for the crime of Nearly Causing Pneumonia and Acting Ridiculous, and I Can't Believe I Had to Send That Poor Boy Home Soaking Wet, What Were You Thinking, Sometimes I Think You Are Crazy, you find yourself sentenced to Apologize to Your Daughter and That Poor Boy.

Apologize! This is unacceptable. Fathers do not apologize to teenage boys. You will Not Under Any Circumstances apologize to anyone and how do you "almost catch pneumonia" anyway? That's like saying someone is "almost pregnant," which, by the way, your judicious application of garden hose prevented and no one seems to want to thank you for that. Apology is Out of the Question, and it's not until you see your wife dumping some blankets and a pillow on the living room couch that you begin to reconsider your position.

When Blunt arrives the next day, you steel yourself for the distasteful task at hand. You remind yourself that you gave your mother-in-law a brief, dry kiss at your wedding; surely you can handle this.

Blunt knocks on the front door a little more hesitantly than usual. (When he first started "going out" or whatever it is that he's been doing to your daughter, he used to just walk in and call out, "Hello, Mr. Cameron!" like a common house burglar, but you discouraged this behavior by politely placing your hands on his shoulders and shoving him back outside.)

Now you open the door and he gives a little start, nervously eyeing you as if checking for weapons. It's enough to make you weep: you finally have this boy where you want him, and your wife wants you to unwind all of your progress by apologizing!

"Hello," you greet him.

"Hello, Mr. Cameron," he replies.

There, that should cover it. You step aside to let him in, as you do so catching sight of your wife standing in the kitchen, shaking her head sternly.

You reflect that another night on that couch and your back will fuse into one giant warp.

"So . . . I guess the other night I sort of sprayed you with the hose," you apologize.

Blunt shrugs uncomfortably.

You glance at your wife, who is still frowning at you. *What more does the woman want?*

Okay, you can do this. "I'm . . ." You choke a little, your throat closing in the involuntary reflex fathers have developed to prevent accidental apologies. "I'm sorry I did that."

"Oh, that's okay, Mr. Cameron. You should see my father when my sister's boyfriend comes over. He still pretends he doesn't remember the guy's name!"

The Potential In-Laws

Despite my stated disinclination to meet the two people whose irresponsible mating resulted in my daughter having a boyfriend, my wife plunged on with her giddy plans for a "family get-together" with Blunt's parents.

I mentally formed an image of what these people might be like, borrowing heavily from the natural history museum's Cro-Magnon man display. They'd grin shamelessly at Blunt's inappropriate behavior around my daughter, the wife openly stating she'd like to see a grandchild soon, like within nine months. "We don't mind at all that she's not even Blunt's cousin," the idiot woman would beam. The father, if he even *is* the father, would drink all my beer and shout ridiculous political arguments at everybody, precisely as my wife has accused me of behaving in the past even though I've never really done such a thing. My sublimely civilized behavior in contrast to this lout would serve as instruction to my children, who would come to appreciate how lucky they were to have me as the head of the family. Eventually, the father's comportment would become so boorish I'd have to drag the man out into the yard and administer a good thrashing. (I pictured having an English accent as I told him what I was doing. "I say there, old boy, I do believe I'm going to have to give you a box about the ears, if you don't mind.")

When they arrived at the front door, they actually appeared a little bit less like cave dwellers than I'd imagined. In fact, Blunt's father looked rather like me, except a lot bigger. I began to rethink the thrashing plan, though I decided I would hang on to the British accent.

"Jolly good, then!" I hailed them. "Come on in, old boy, come in. There there. Cheerio."

My wife gaped at me.

"Dad! Why are you faking a speech impediment!" my daughter hissed as we ushered the couple into the house.

We accepted an apple pie that Blunt's mother had made herself. "Wow, I wish my wife could bake apple pie," I sighed wistfully. My wife gave me an entirely different sort of look.

Naturally, my daughter and Blunt had to greet each

other as if he had been missing at sea for a year. I noticed his father looking away in embarrassment, not meeting my eyes, while the two women glowed.

The father's name was Ted Petersen. We opened a couple of beers and went out on the back deck to engage in manly conversation. "I pretty much built this deck myself. Watch yourself there, the railing is a little loose," I told him. "Well, don't worry about it, I'll nail it back in place later, just let it lie there."

"I'm impressed," Ted said, looking around at my handiwork. "You did a great job."

"At what?" my wife demanded, emerging from the kitchen and handing me a platter of hamburgers.

"At building the deck," Ted explained.

My wife snorted. "What? All he did was put up that railing. My father built the rest of it."

I gave Ted a shrug of the shoulders. If she wanted to believe that her father built my back deck, I wasn't going to argue with her. To my way of thinking, however, all my father-in-law did was cut up the wood and hammer it in place, while I handled the architectural drawings.

"What do you do with your spare time, Ted?" I asked.

"I teach karate to children down at the YMCA," he answered.

I decided that any lingering thoughts I'd had about that thrashing were no longer valid. I put the meat on the grill, frowning thoughtfully. "Is Blunt your only child?" I inquired after a moment.

He frowned. "Who?"

I gestured with my spatula, spattering Ted with a little hamburger juice. "Him."

He looked over at his son. "Oh, Blaine? No, he has an older sister."

"Does she have a boyfriend?" I asked pleasantly.

"Well, I'm not sure."

"Let me put it another way. Is there a particular boy who seems to hang around at your house all the time?"

"Yes! I can't seem to get rid of him!"

"I see . . . Well, let me ask you this. Does he eat all of your food?"

"At least four hundred dollars a week in groceries!" Ted's eyes lit up with relief at being able to talk to someone about this at last. "His name is Mutt. Mutt Crumplefungus."

His wife's head snapped around. "Are you talking about Matt?" she demanded.

He nodded.

"His name is Matt Gundlefinger," she corrected sternly.

We men stood together in silent condemnation of a name like that, while she turned back to my wife and proclaimed, "He's such a *nice* boy."

"Well, Ted, it sounds to me like you've been infected with a boyfriend," I diagnosed sadly.

He nodded morosely.

"Have you checked into Our Lady of Suffering Nunnery?"

"That in Indiana?"

"Yep."

He shrugged. "I just don't know what to do, Bruce."

I found myself rather liking the old boy, all of a sudden: he wasn't a bad sod at all, what?

Oral Arguments

At some point, your daughter will decide to demonstrate her total control over the boyfriend, dragging him shocked and bewildered into their "first fight."

While cheering may seem appropriate, fathers are urged to restrain their enthusiasm. This is difficult, however, when you see the expression on the boyfriend's face—he looks like he's lost three quarts of blood. (If you're not accustomed to a woman's tactics, arguing with one can be very disquieting.)

My own wife, as an example, has established a rather bizarre pattern of behavior whenever I go to the sports bar to be with my friends for a few hours. Despite the fact that I have absolutely no control over how long the game lasts, and despite the fact that she is by now very aware that the minute one game is over something else comes on the TV, like Australian football or California sand polo, and despite the fact that I have my buddies telephone her and make up hilarious excuses as to why I am so late, often referring in good-natured humor to buxom waitresses and other such jovial matters, she still persists in throwing my clothes out the upstairs window and into the bushes in the front yard. The first couple of times the taxi dropped me off and I spotted what appeared to be the work of an insane laundress, I was not really sure what was going on, and her refusal to open the bedroom door to talk about it didn't help any. Now, though, I understand we are "arguing," and I actually have found the whole process helpful—even though I'm locked out of my own room, I still have plenty of things to change into in the morning. (I've learned to pick up the clothes when I arrive home. If I leave them out, the women in the neighborhood will see the clothes and then *they* will refuse to talk to me. The men, however, will come over, look at the clothes, and ask how the game turned out.)

When I came upon Blunt standing forlornly on our front

porch, I didn't need a bunch of boxer shorts in the bushes to tell me he was having a fight with my older daughter. One look at the devastation on his face revealed the whole story.

"Mr. Cameron," he greeted me, "we're having a fight."

"Sorry to hear that," I chuckled. "You know, my daughter can really carry a lifetime grudge."

He sighed, nodding.

"Maybe you should give it time to cool off. The rest of the school year, as an example," I advised kindly.

He sagged onto the porch swing. "It's my fault."

"Sure it is," I encouraged. I had no desire to find out what lay at the heart of this dispute, but I was eager to re-inforce the idea that he had damaged his relationship beyond repair. "You're old enough to join the army, aren't you?"

"I didn't say 'Sugar Bear,'" he added.

This stopped me. "I . . . what?"

"She says, 'That's sweet,' and I'm supposed to answer, 'Sure is, Sugar Bear.'"

"Ah. Listen, I have to go."

"And she said it was because I was looking at the wait-ress."

"I see. Well, were you?"

"Huh?"

"Were you looking at the waitress?"

He shrugged. "A little."

"Ah."

"What am I going to do? She's really pissed."

"Well," I said kindly, "I think you've pretty much blown it with this one. You should go out and find yourself another daughter. I mean, another girlfriend."

I went inside, shutting the door behind me in a manner that I hoped suggested eternal banishment. My daughter was on the phone, talking to one Heather or another about something besides Blunt for the first time in thirty days.

Most fathers would assume that for the crime of too much waitress and not enough Sugar Bear, the boyfriend would be permanently excommunicated. Alas, these storms blow through teenage relationships rather quickly, and before long they are "making up," an entirely inappropriate process that has everyone but you sighing in relief. "I'm glad they could work it out," your wife will murmur, watching your daughter and Blunt nuzzle each other. I'm sure if your wife were Winston Churchill she probably would have said, "I'm glad Hitler and Stalin could get over their differences and destroy Poland."

Conclusion

The main difference between a "date" and a "boyfriend" is that dates are in your daughters' lives but boyfriends are in *everybody's* lives. He's there for dinner, he starts appearing in holiday photographs—you'll even find your wife buying him a birthday gift *from you*. "He really likes you," your wife will remark one day.

You do not want to be liked, you want to be *feared*.

There are countries, I am told, where the whole boyfriend stage is considered a waste of time—fathers pick sons-in-law out of a lineup, basing their selection on such attributes as the boy's ability to help out on the farm. Now, I don't have a farm, but I certainly would be willing to get one in order to implement this logical system.

When you find yourself infested with a boyfriend, there isn't much you can do to get rid of him—not legally, anyway. But take heart: even the nicest boy will eventually be tossed out like clothes into the bushes on a Saturday night—teenage girls don't do stability.

At some point, you'll encounter a boy who actually wants to *marry* your child, sort of an extreme manifestation of the boyfriend problem. Hopefully, though, that event is many years away. The thing to do now is instill in your daughter's mind that it is "romantic" for any suitor to ask *you* for permission to propose to her. That way, when the time comes, you'll have some say in the matter. That's only appropriate: you're the father.

The High Cost of Higher Education

A Father Is Called Upon to Pay for an Expensive Four-Year Vacation

Despite the fact that magazine articles have been warning you since your children were babies that you need to be setting aside at least 75 percent of your disposable income for future college tuition, you've somehow failed to adequately prepare yourself for the financial train wreck of higher education. (They call it disposable income, so you disposed of it. Where's the surprise?) Now you're starting to receive "College Cost Calculators" in the mail, and whoever writes these things has Stephen King beat hands down for their ability to cause you to wake up screaming.

"We may need to cut back on certain discretionary items," your wife suggests.

"Like protein," you agree. "And housing."

"I'll sleep in my tent!" your son volunteers.

You might be more enthusiastic about the investment you'll be making if you saw any signs that college was part of a long-range career plan. Maybe if your daughter would say, "I'm going into risk management and hope to earn enough by the time I'm thirty to buy my dad a condo in

Hawaii," you'd be able to face the cost projections with something besides nausea. But all she seems to be able to say for sure about her future is that she will be joining a sorority. At this point, the whole purpose of college appears to be social.

"I'd rather have my fingernails pulled out than be in a sorority," your younger daughter sneers.

"My nails are professionally done," your older daughter brags. "They're acrylic."

One reason to look forward to your daughter going to college: you won't have to listen to any more conversations like this.

Operating under a deadline, you present your daughter with a brilliant four-point program for paying for college:

1. Army
2. Air force
3. Navy
4. Marines

"Oh, I'm *sure* I'd join the army," your daughter snarls while you seductively hum "Be All That You Can Be."

Your wife lends her opinion: "Absolutely not. I will not have my child fighting in combat."

"They don't engage in combat," you object. "Haven't you seen the commercials? All they do is climb ropes and stuff."

"Oh, I'm sure I'd climb a *rope*," your older daughter sniffs.

"You might break an acrylic nail," your other daughter observes.

"They'll pay thousands of dollars toward college," you explain. "I think it is worth exploring, finding out more about it. Can we at least compromise on that point?"

"Absolutely not," your wife compromises.

So it's all up to you: not only paying for this expensive education-without-end-goal, but as events will reveal, doing all the work to ensure your daughter gets into college in the first place.

Two Approaches to Getting into College

In order for your daughter to attend college, three things must happen. All three of these require continuous intervention by the father: (*a*) she must score reasonably well on her SATs; (*b*) she must apply to a college; and (*c*) she must graduate from high school. Here are the differences between a father's approach to these three goals, and a teenage daughter's approach.

Activity

Earn an acceptable score on the SATs

Father's Approach

1. Purchase several study guides.

2. Spend six weeks poring over study guides.

3. Turn every dinner into a TV game show format, asking questions about grammar and geometry, awarding points for correct answers.

4. Write sample questions on flash cards and leave them strategically placed around the house.

Daughter's Approach

1. Ignore the study guide.

2. Refuse to play the game at dinner.

3. Ignore the flash cards.

4. Ignore the father.

5. The night before the test, stay up until 2 A.M. crying with a friend who got dumped by a boyfriend.

6. Oversleep the morning of SATs.

7. Refuse to talk to the father about how the test went.

Activity

Apply to college

Father's Approach

1. Order 120 college catalogues.

2. Categorize them according to expense.

3. Put each school in a manila folder, recording important selection factors on the cover.

4. Rank the colleges in order of appeal and review daily, even hourly.

5. Apply to all of those that don't require an application fee.

6. Compile a list of famous alumni from each school. Investigate each school's academic record. Ponder factors such as cost, endowment size, age of facilities, cost, reputation, cost, and cost.

Daughter's Approach

1. Ignore all 120 catalogues.

2. Find out where best friends are applying and apply there.

3. Select the school with the prettiest campus that is also located near (a) the beach, (b) a major ski resort, or (c) Disney World.

Activity

Graduate

Father's Approach

1. Urge the daughter to spend extra hours studying in those subjects where academic performance has been weakest—namely, the academic subjects.

2. Require a daily report to father on progress in problem areas.

3. Endlessly discuss the issue of extra credit.

Daughter's Approach

1. Ignore the father.

2. Call Heather, Amanda, Margi, and Brooke every single night and talk for hours about anything except school.

3. Ignore homework assignments and looming tests.

4. Somehow, despite the lack of effort, squeak by.

Preparing for the SATs

When the first SAT study guide arrives it is as thick as the maintenance manual for the space shuttle. You can't wait to open it: before your daughter even gets home you've prepared a list of questions to drill her with. This is going to be fun!

"How about a question on accumulating percentages?" you greet her as she walks in the door. She arrests her reflexive reach for the telephone, staring at you as if you've gone mad. Perhaps it *is* an odd way to start a conversation, but you plunge on. "Suppose you purchase two items on sale at the mall."

Now *this* is something she's interested in. "Go on," she says cautiously.

"The first item costs twenty-five dollars, but it is on sale for fifty percent off," you continue. "The second item is twenty-five percent off. How much would the nonsale price of the second item need to be in order to save one hundred percent of the nonsale price of the first item?" Your lips move as you reread the question to yourself. Does this even make any sense?

"Wait a minute. You can save one hundred percent?" she demands.

"Right. The combined total of the savings on the two items would have to add up to the nonsale price of the first."

"Well, obviously it is a trick question."

"I beg your pardon?"

"If something's that cheap, it's probably completely out of style."

"Let's just pretend here."

"Okay." She shrugs. "Twenty-five dollars?"

That sounds good to you, too, but when you look up the answer, you shake your head and cluck. "Wrong!"

"Whatever."

"Remember, you've already saved twelve dollars and fifty cents on the original item."

"This would never happen in real life."

"Sure it would!"

"Well then, I would just return the items," she snaps. "They don't make you do *math* when you buy things. That's why they have cash registers."

"The answer is that the second item would need to have a total nonsale cost of fifty dollars," you inform her pontifically. You hope she'll take your word for this because you're not sure you can explain it.

"Whatever."

"Let's do history."

"Oh, I'm *not* doing history!"

"Where was the battle of Gettysburg fought?" you prod. "I'll give you a hint, it begins with a *G*."

"I'm against all wars and will refuse to answer any questions that have to do with the killing of human beings."

"It rhymes with 'Betty's Slurg,'" you offer seductively.

"I'm going to my room."

"Hey, how about Gettysburg?" you propose. "Make sense?"

"Go away!"

"How about the battle of the Bulge, where was that fought? Here's a hint, it was not fought in a place called Bulge."

"There are no history questions on the SAT," she states.

"Ha!" you answer. "Take a look at this!" She stands with her arms folded while you flip through the study guide, your wrist sagging under its weight. "It's right here," you declare, still looking. When you glance up, your daughter is wearing a triumphant expression.

"Told you."

"Clearly this is a defective guide."

"Dad, our teachers say they don't do history!"

How can that be? Have we really gotten to a point in our society where the Civil War is less important than what is on sale at the mall? You shake your head, sure that when *you* took the SATs, it was loaded with history questions.

Obviously, the SATs were much more difficult when you were a teenager.

The Application Essay—
Torture for the Whole Family

Though she declares it the "dumbest waste of a Saturday I ever heard of," your daughter manages to do a decent job on her SATs, leading to the next step: applying for college. When she realizes this isn't a simple matter of having her dad send off some money and a small form, she becomes angry at *you*. "Why do I have to answer all these questions?" she demands, outraged.

She becomes even more furious when she realizes she must write an application essay. "Don't these people realize I have better things to do?" she complains. One essay asks her to describe her reading preferences.

"I think you should put something besides *In Style* magazine," you suggest helpfully over her shoulder. "They're probably looking for books."

"I don't have time to read books, I'm a high school senior!"

This is so discouraging you lack the strength to answer.

Another school requests her to pen something on her writing style. "Writing an essay on how you write an essay is like painting a picture to show how you paint," she storms.

"You can always just pursue a career in food service," you remind her. "No one says you *have* to go to college."

Your wife gives you a warning look, but clearly you're just being masterfully psychological, because your daughter finally shuts up and starts working on her application essays. This requires everyone in the house to be absolutely silent. "Can you please be quiet, I am working on my essay!" she shrieks at the slightest noise. "You have no idea how hard this is!"

If walking around on tiptoes for a few days will get her moved out of the house, everyone in the family seems to feel it is worth it.

Coasting Toward Graduation

"Senioritis" is a word used to describe the attitude a high school student takes toward academics in the final months of the final school year. It comes from the word "senior," which means "superior to," and "itis," which means "swollen or inflamed." So you're living with this superior-acting, swollen high schooler who no longer sees the need to open her textbooks, which will absolutely inflame you. "It's just not relevant," she sighs, rolling her eyes. "I won't use any of this stuff in the real world."

"What stuff? Math? English? What sort of work are you planning to do?" you demand.

"I don't know yet, but it won't involve math or English," she vows.

"Maybe you could stand in the road with a sign that says 'Slow,'" you suggest helpfully. "No wait, the word 'Slow' is written in English."

"Can I do that job when I grow up, Dad?" your son asks eagerly. "I've always wanted to do that."

Finally, without any visible evidence of studying and despite your dire predictions, your daughter graduates. This is a process that involves much weeping. Everyone starts hugging as if there has been an earthquake, and hordes of teenagers descend like locusts to deplete your food supply and your reserves of sleep.

The commencement ceremony starts with a volley of soporific speeches that sound suspiciously like the exact same orations delivered when *you* graduated. As you fight off REM, you're treated to a mind-numbing march of strangers, all ridiculously garbed, trailing like learned ants up to retrieve their documents and return to their seats. Four hours into the event, you ponder whether it would be worth it to fake a fight with the guy sitting behind you so the two of you could be thrown out of the place.

Then finally the point of the whole show: your daughter makes her appearance. You watch through the video camera as she mounts the steps, takes her diploma (until this moment you thought it was possible the principal would shake his head and say, "Sorry, you should have studied more, as your father said"), and vanishes off the stage.

She also vanishes from your control. She is, after all, a high school graduate, and eighteen years old to boot: rules no longer should apply. "I'm going to be in college!" she rages when you tell her that if she lives in your house, she must do as you say. "I can't believe you still think I have curfew."

Another area of contention surfaces immediately, when it becomes obvious that you and your daughter have differing ideas on how she should spend the next three months.

The summer after high school is a critical time in a teenage girl's life, a brief but rich opportunity for saving money for college. This will never happen. Your daughter is now having "the last summer vacation where I won't have to work," as she'll put it.

"What do you mean you don't have to work? Who said you don't have to work?" you'll demand.

"You think this is easy?" she'll cry. "These are my best friends in the whole world and I will never have a chance to see them again."

If you point out that this is ridiculous, she's going to college with half of them—she and Heather have vowed to join the same sorority, even—everyone in the family will pretend you're being mean.

"I need to borrow some money. We're having a farewell party at Margi's house tonight," she says to you. In this context, "borrow" means the same as "remove."

"Didn't you have a farewell party last night?"

"That was at Amanda's house."

"But aren't these the same exact people? Don't you understand the meaning of the word 'farewell'? It means 'I won't see you for a long time, so fare thee well.' You don't keep saying farewell to each other every night for a month."

Your daughter starts wiping at tears in her eyes. "Don't say that. This can't be for a long time. These are like the most important people in my whole life. I'll see my friends again, I know I will!"

"I know you will too. You'll see them tomorrow night, when you have another farewell party," you reply.

Your wife is shooting you the Look. Recognizing defeat, you pull out your wallet. "These were the best dollars of my life and I'll never see them again," you announce lugubriously. No one laughs.

Congratulations!
Let the Cash Depletion Begin!

Your daughter treats her college acceptance with as much interest as she does your description of your day at work.

You've been anxiously flipping through the mail every day, fretting over the lack of any response from the college of choice, when your daughter mentions offhandedly that she was accepted two weeks ago via e-mail.

Your congratulations are shrugged off—apparently Heather also got in, but prospects are not as promising for Burke. Heather refuses to go to college without someone to break up with once she gets there, and your daughter refuses to go without Heather.

Meanwhile, the school, utterly unconcerned about such earthshaking matters, begins asking for money. Lots of it. You inquire about financial assistance, and the envelope from the Department of Student Aid that arrives in response appears to hold promise, until it becomes clear that the only "aid" you're going to get is a "loan." You've been trying to turn away this sort of philanthropy from credit card companies for years, but you reluctantly realize you're not going to fulfill your lifelong ambition of seeing Heather, Burke, and your daughter go to college without borrowing some money.

To obtain this "aid," you must first qualify, and the school helpfully provides you with a form to assist you in doing so.

Eligibility for College Loan

Making it possible for parents to enjoy paying for college long after their children have graduated.

Step 1	List your annual income.	$ _____
Step 2	*Send it to us.*	
Step 3	State the liquidation value of the total of your household assets.	$ _____
Step 4	*Send it to us.*	
Step 5	State the total combined amount of the UNUSED portion of any credit lines.	$ _____
Step 6	*Send it to us.*	
Step 7	Congratulations! You qualify for a college loan. Please sign the attached "Contract for Lifelong Indebtedness" and the "I'll Never Be Able to Retire" statement.	
Step 8	*Send it to us.*	

It's a good thing you've applied for a loan, because you quickly discover that higher learning is a matter of room, board, tuition, and a bunch of expenses you've never heard of.

EXPENSIVE UNIVERSITY

Dear Mr. Cameron:

Please endorse a check for $785.00 for the following fees for your incoming student:

$ 80	Special event participation fee
$ 80	Special event nonparticipation fee
$125	Anticipation of excess dryer lint fee
$200	"No Dogs Allowed" signage fee
$100	"Except Seeing Eye Dogs" signage fee
$100	Disposal of nonrecyclable items fee
$100	Nondisposal of nonrecyclable items fee
$100	Fee to process your check for these fees

Yours truly,

Dean of Department of Expenses You've Never Heard Of

When Burke is finally accepted, you half expect a letter of congratulations from the school, but their computers are working overtime spitting out notices to you on other weighty matters, such as whether you'll become a member of the Screaming Geezers, a group of fathers who attend college athletic events and, well, scream. It ony costs $500 to become a Geezer, a development you had heretofore thought was sort of automatic at some point.

Meanwhile, you're grappling with issues of your own. You find yourself dashing off a letter to the college, hoping to resolve your concerns. They write back immediately:

EXPENSIVE UNIVERSITY

Dear Mr. Cameron:

   In response to your question, no, it is not true that "everybody will have a car at college," as your daughter states. Only those students whose parents truly love them will have a car at college.

   If you have any more questions, please do not hesitate to contact me.

                    Sincerely,

                    Dean of Panicky Last-Minute Anxieties

Off to College

The countdown for the drive to college begins about a week before the actual departure, with a flurry of shopping. Apparently higher education requires a new wardrobe. Feeling ravaged by the bills you've *already* paid, you mention some concerns you have about such topics as bankruptcy and starvation, but you are either ignored or frowned upon for being mean.

Naturally, it's up to you to load the car. As you pack, you're amazed at what has been purchased: a case of granola bars; enough Q-Tips to keep her ears clean not only through college, but through medical school as well; a tub of petroleum jelly she could swim in.

The drive itself makes you glad the word "manic" was invented so you'd have a way to describe your daughter's chatter. She and your wife speculate on what they will need to buy. "Curtains," they decide. "Something to hang on the walls. House plants. Oh, and what about one of those hand-held vacuums?"

"What about Q-Tips?" you inquire in a surly tone. You're ignored.

"Ohmygod, Mom, I don't have a bookshelf!" your daughter squeals.

"Make a list," your wife urges.

THE HIGH COST OF HIGHER EDUCATION

"Okay. Curtains. Bookshelf. Gas fireplace. One of those mirror balls that hang over the dance floors in discos. Bearskin rug. Zamboni," she chants, your wife nodding approvingly.

She quiets down, though, when the campus looms up ahead. Although she's seen it before, it was always as a prospective student, not as a new tenant, and the thought of spending the next several years here without family seems to diminish her enthusiasm a little.

Her room is a bit spartan. Clearly the person who designed the place intended it to serve as a bomb shelter at some point. The cinder-block walls defy anyone to hang artwork, which causes you to brighten slightly—you had the impression, coming down, that your wife was going to go out and purchase a Monet. The room is different from a prison cell in that it lacks bars on the window, and you're not sure how you feel about that. You fret over the omnipresence of boys wandering the halls—you knew the dorm was coed, but does that mean there have to be boys?

Your wife grabs the list and the car keys and runs out to find a store, muttering about "sprucing the place up." Your suggestion that maybe your daughter should live in the room for a while, see what she needs before anything more is purchased, is completely ignored.

Time for registration. The same stubborn little girl

who used to take two hours to tie her shoes because she didn't want anyone to help her now seems reluctant to leave your side. Without touching you, she seems to be clinging. "Registration is over there," you point out.

"I know!" she snaps. You do a mental review of the debt you have taken on in order to get her to this point and decide her hostility is misplaced. But a glance at the stress on her face convinces you to withhold criticism for now—you're sure there will be plenty of opportunity for criticism later.

"Here we are. Let's get in line," you suggest.

She whirls on you. "No! You stay here. I'll do it myself."

"But . . ."

"Stay . . . here," she hisses through clenched teeth. Then, bracing herself, she stalks over to wait in line.

You look around for someone to complain to and spot a group of dads standing around in a discarded fashion. You walk over and nod at them.

"She says she wants to do it herself," you explain. They all smile sadly.

"I have a hernia from carrying my daughter's Strato-lounger into her room," one man complains.

"My son took my television," states another.

"I've met my daughter's roommate and can't tell what sex it is."

"Why do they call them *student* loans if it is the *parent* who signs for them?"

"Four years of competitive soccer league and then she doesn't even want to apply for a scholarship. Says she's *bored* with soccer."

"My son's bicycle cost more than my car."

"My wife went shopping for more spruce for the room," you tell them.

They all nod.

"Mine too. Shopping," says the one with the hernia.

"Shopping," they all agree.

Your daughter appears at your elbow. "Dad! I need a two-hundred-dollar library security deposit!" She appears angry with you that she has to ask you for money. You write out the check and she snatches it from your hand.

About the third time she approaches you for a check, you've had it. "I'll go up with you," you say firmly.

She pales. "But Dad . . ."

"I either stand next to you or there will be no more help from me, this day of checks without balances. No more money for boat storage fees or dog wash or mirror alignment or whatever else these vampires want. You are either on your own or I am with you. Your choice."

She bites her lip but allows you to get in the next line with her. Her posture is wooden, clearly communicating to the rest of the world that she doesn't know you and considers you invisible. You reach out and, to her shock, slip an arm around her shoulders, which tense palpably with your touch. "With me or on your own," you repeat.

The group of dads nods approvingly.

By the end of the afternoon your checkbook is depleted. You figure one of your first tasks upon returning home will be to call the bank and negotiate your surrender.

The Good-bye

When I took my older daughter to college, I was so focused on the logistical task of moving her belongings, I didn't really think about what I was *really* doing: moving her out of my life and into the start of hers. After spending the last half decade prowling the house at night, wondering where she was and what she was doing and with whom she was doing it, we were now entering a phase where I would never know these things. No curfew, no way to interview and fail her dates, no opportunity to offer constructive criticism when needed, which was, in my opinion, constantly.

Looking at my daughter, I saw my little girl in a woman's body, tall and strong but unfinished, not ready. Or maybe it was I who was not ready—I certainly felt unsure as she walked us to the parking lot for the final good-bye. How was this natural, to drive my daughter to this strange place, write fifty checks, and then drive away, leaving her in the hands of strangers with whom I shared nothing but the contents of my bank account? Her whole life I had protected her from harm, a job that did not in any way feel done.

I tried to give her some advice in a rush. "Walk to each of your classes before the first day," I told her. "Time yourself so you know how long it takes. Get up and eat breakfast every morning, no matter what." These are things I never did myself.

She nodded, grateful, I think, not for the words, which she would ignore anyway, but the act itself, a familiar ritual for her to cling to in an otherwise alien experience.

And then we were there by the car. My wife hugged her and sobbed as if our daughter were leaving on a boat for the New World.

"Write," my wife urged.

"I'll write," my daughter agreed.

"Call."

"I'll call."

"Study," I suggested. No one responded.

When it was my turn I pulled her to me and concentrated on remaining dry eyed. The words I wanted to say could not fight their way past the tight constriction in my throat, and when I felt the press of her lips against my cheek, I had to look away.

I did manage to say something, I think, before sliding numbly into the front seat and starting the minivan. My daughter's little wave was harder for me than the last hug—a tentative but somehow reassuring flicker of her fingers. I found myself remembering her waving at me from the front window when I would leave for work in the morning, when she was not just my first but my only child.

She stood in the parking lot and watched us as we eased slowly down the road. I kept my eye on the rearview mirror and watched her shrink against the backdrop of the college campus, until she seemed so forlornly insignificant it was all I could do to keep from wheeling around to make sure she was still there.

I settled in for the drive, smiling so my wife wouldn't think I was weeping, and tried not to dwell on the odd stillness in the car caused by my daughter's absence.

My wife and I didn't talk much on the way home. Though the nest would hardly be empty when we got there, we were entering a new phase of life now, the start of a process of letting our children go. Neither of us was sure how this would affect our lives, but then, we hadn't known what would happen when we decided to have kids in the first place.

"I miss her already," my wife murmured after a bit.

I did too. And I knew that our daughter wouldn't really be writing and calling every day. Our oldest has always been independent, has always made it clear she wanted to be in charge of her own life. I imagined that if we weren't the ones to call, it would be a long time before we heard from her.

Then the cell phone rang. My wife answered it, since we have a policy against me crashing the car while I'm driving it.

"Oh, honey," my wife said after a moment. "I understand. I know it can be difficult."

I sent her a questioning look, and she made a sad face.

"I'm sure you'll be okay, dear," she responded after a long silence. "Honestly, it is going to be all right."

They spoke for a few more minutes, and then my wife hung up with a thoughtful look on her face.

"Is our college girl homesick already?" I asked sympathetically.

She shook her head. "No. She says she's the only person in her dorm without her own credit card."

"Oh," I answered. I digested this for a few miles. "And I take it that she thinks this is somehow something that I'm supposed to fix?"

"Of course," my wife answered smoothly. "You're the father."

ACKNOWLEDGMENTS

Thanks to my Internet subscribers, whose devotion and willingness to pass along the Cameron Column helped make it popular and convinced me maybe I should keep writing humor after all.

Thanks to my longtime friend Paul Dalen for volunteering to create and maintain the first Cameron Web site.

Thanks to the picky, picky proofreader of my column, Bob Bridges, for helping me dot eyes and cross tees.

Were it not for my agent, Jody Rein, no one in the print world would ever have heard of W. Bruce Cameron. You really are the best, Jody.

Most of the administrative tasks of maintaining my Internet newsletter are handled by my volunteer staff, who turns out to be my mother. Thanks for all your help, Mom.

Special thanks to John Temple and Mary Winter of the Denver *Rocky Mountain News*, who took a chance and made me their humor columnist.

Few writers are given the opportunity to work with an editor like Margot Herrera, who was gentle and wise throughout the entire rewrite and rewrite and rewrite process. I'm very grateful to have had the opportunity to work with her.

And naturally, I am deeply indebted to my two teenage daughters for driving me crazy enough to write a book about it.